99 WAYS

TO START A

STUDY
GROUP

And Keep It Growing

BOOKS BY LAWRENCE O. RICHARDS

The Believer's Guidebook
The Believer's Praise Book
The Believer's Prayer Book
The Believer's Promise Book
The Christian Man's Promise Book
The Christian Woman's Promise Book
Creative Personal Bible Study
Dictionary of Basic Bible Truths
Expository Dictionary of Bible Words
Love Your Neighbor: A Woman's Workshop on Fellowship
Practical Theology of Spirituality
A Theology of Children's Ministry
A Theology of Christian Education
Youth Ministry: Its Renewal in the Local Church
A Theology of Church Leadership (with Clyde Hoeldtke)
A Theology of Personal Ministry (with Gib Martin)

99 WAYS
TO START A
STUDY GROUP
And Keep It Growing

Lawrence O. Richards

Lamplighter Books Grand Rapids, Michigan
Zondervan Publishing House

99 WAYS TO START A STUDY GROUP AND KEEP IT GROWING
Revised edition copyright © 1987 by Lawrence O. Richards.

Lamplighter Books are published by the Zondervan Publishing House
1415 Lake Drive, S.E., Grand Rapids, Michigan 49506

First published under the title *Sixty-nine Ways to Start a Study Group and Keep It Growing.*
Copyright © 1973 by the Zondervan Corporation.

Library of Congress Cataloging in Publication Data

Richards, Larry, 1931–
    99 ways to start a study group and keep it growing.

    Revised ed. of: Sixty-nine ways to start a study group and keep it
growing. © 1973.
    1. Bible—Study. 2. Church group work. I. Richards, Larry,
1931–. 69 ways to start a study group and keep it growing. II. Title.
III. Title: Ninety-nine ways to start a study group and keep it
growing.
BS600.2.R517 1987   259'.7   87-14779
ISBN 0-310-31921-8

Printed in the United States of America

87 88 89 90 91 / CH / 10 9 8 7 6 5 4 3 2 1

Contents

1. Meet for Ministry   7

Part 1—Principles of Group Ministry

2. Identification   22

3. Affirmation   37

4. Exploration   53

5. Concentration   68

6. Adoration   81

Part 2—Action Ideas   87

Stuart Proctor

1

meet for ministry

The lady in Detroit was very positive. I was speaking to a Sunday school staff about the role of interpersonal relationships in teaching, and she reacted. "That sounds like 'small-group' talk. I'd rather hear a well-prepared teacher lecture. I've been in groups for the past four years, and it's just a sharing of ignorance."

I could sympathize. I've been in disappointing groups, too. I've been in groups who came together because some of us felt a need, but somehow that need was never met.

I'm afraid many small groups that Christians form turn out this way. As the weeks of meetings go by, members are somehow disappointed. Something seems to be missing.

Yet, I've talked with other Christians who have had positive and exciting experiences in their groups. I myself have experienced rewarding times when God has met us and significantly changed the lives of members of our small group. For many years I served as an elder in a congregation that was actually built around "little churches," small groups that met during the week. For our congregation the dynamic of those little churches made a constant impact, not just on individuals, but on the vitality of our church as well.

Over the years I've come to a simple conclusion. Small groups of Christians meeting together can succeed, but they can also fail. There's no magic in "small groups." Yet, when we do meet with others in a smaller, sharing group of believers and when we *meet for ministry* rather than for "Bible study," God does work in exciting and positive ways.

Words of testimony

Listen to a few comments from members of a small-ministry group I helped begin but was not part of. What, of everything these folks say, would you most want from small-group participation?

From Bill

The group has been a blessing for both Carol and me. We've come to love each member a great deal. The sharing, reflecting, and applying by the group has led me to realize the importance of mutual ministry. For twenty-three years I led a life of complete darkness. What a joy to glimpse truth as Christ reveals himself to me through the eyes and understanding of the whole group.

The most outstanding point about our group is the fact that whatever we study in Acts applies to our lives directly. It's a highlight for me when each of us shares what the passages say to our lives. We often come to the point where we give our testimonies, share daily problems, and talk about conflicts. This sharing has brought the group closer together and binds us to one another in Christ.

The effectiveness of our group doesn't rest on the Bible study alone. There's the fellowship we have during the rest of the week—in our homes, over the phone—that brings us closer together. I'm applying

God's Word to my life and getting support from other Christians who really care that I continue to grow.

From Nancy

One advantage of being in a group Bible study is motivation. Reading Acts, knowing that I will be sharing my findings with others, makes me begin to dig. I need to dig because I've spent ten odd years without ever making the Bible part of my everyday life. Somehow I've missed out learning self-discipline in reading the Scripture, and especially in praying. Having a group of others to share with has motivated me, and that's a start.

I don't know whether I'm a hand, a foot, or just a hair on the head, but it's good, good, good to be part of a body. When one part hurts the hand-foot-or-just-hair hurts, too, and when one part sings I hum along too!

From Barb

I'm not here primarily to cram my head with some knowledge about the Bible. I think I'm here because God wants me to learn in a fuller way how he is working in people's lives and changing the world today. Theory is fun—and I really get excited about how things fit together. But what excites me more is realizing that we aren't just studying about the church—the body of Christ—we *are* the body of Christ.

One of the most important things for me is that I am beginning to assume that God is really working in us, and I find myself expectantly watching to see what is happening.

I do not see small groups as necessarily the answer to all the world's problems. But I do know that right now these people who are praying for me, supporting me, loving me, are people whom I trust and love with my very being. God *is* using them to change me, although it isn't a very rapid change. And I can see how others are changing as well, not into a mold, but freer to become themselves. I've found that the interest I have in them, and how God is working in their lives, is important for my vision of the world. I really love them. And *that* is pretty neat.

It's exciting for me to see God work in the lives of people who meet for ministry. Bill, Nancy, Barb, and all the others who have discovered how to open hearts to each other and to God are learning something that is basic to our Christian faith. Like them, I want to continue meeting for ministry because I know that when I do I will:

- look at the Bible through other pairs of eyes.
- discover how Scripture applies directly to life.
- apply the Word and get support from others who care that I continue to grow.
- experience Christian love.
- experience Christ's body.
- see change—in my own life and in others.
- be stimulated to worship the Lord truly.
- come to know God in a fresh way and sense his work in my life and in others.

What kind of group

There are many different kinds of "groups" that Christians can become a part of. "Small groups" can be formed for a number of different purposes. For instance, there are action groups that assemble to work on a particular task. There are friendship groups that get together just to enjoy each other's company. There are therapy groups where people meet to talk about deep, personal problems. There are study groups that meet to talk about books they're reading, to listen to and discuss some minister's tapes, or to examine doctrine. There are groups that meet with an evangelistic purpose. All these, coupled with all the committees and boards of a local congregation, are "small groups" of believers.

In each, however, it is not the size of the group that's most significant. It is the *purpose for which the group gathers* that makes it unique.

So, it's important to understand the purpose of the kind of small group this book is about. And it's important to realize that I am not criticizing other kinds of small groups. I'm not at all.

It's just that when Christians are looking for that "something more" to enrich their experience of Jesus, that "something more" to stimulate their personal spiritual growth, there is a *kind* of small group that's best suited to meet their needs. And this is a small group that *meets for ministry*—a kind of special ministry that is in unique harmony with where God himself is going in their lives.

Where *is* God going? When we ask this question, we find some exciting answers in Scripture. Jesus first hints at this in the Sermon on the Mount. After telling those who would listen that their lives are to be marked by an outgoing love, even for enemies (Matt. 5:38–44), Jesus explains that this is only appropriate because God himself treats all with love, and we are to "be sons of your Father in heaven" (5:45). Somehow, because we *are* God's children, it is fitting that we "be perfect, even as your Father in heaven is perfect" (5:48, LIVING BIBLE).

At first it stuns us—this idea that we bear the stamp of God and express him in our lives on earth. But the theme is repeated. Phillips beautifully renders Paul's thought that God has chosen us "to bear the family likeness of his Son, that he might be the eldest of a family of many brothers" (Rom. 8:29). The resem-

11

blance is made possible because salvation brings us more than forgiveness; it brings us *life.* "You are sons of God now," Peter reminds us. "The live, permanent Word of the living God has given you his own indestructible heredity" (1 Peter 1:23, PHILLIPS).

We do have new life.

God's life.

And, in each of us, God is moving in a distinct and unique direction. *God is in the process of forming Christ in our personalities.* He is bringing us to the place where we experience, with Paul, "I have been crucified with Christ and I no longer live, but Christ lives in me. The life I live in the body, I live by faith in the Son of God, who loved me and gave himself for me" (Gal. 2:20).

This is something we need to keep in perspective. God is *not* primarily concerned with what we *do;* God's first concern is who we *are.* For God knows, as the Bible testifies, the more our behavior is like his, the more we will reach out, as Jesus did, to touch people in need, people suffering injustice, people without Christ.

The more we are like Jesus within, the more we will act as he did in our world.

It is this concept of where God is going that gives us our goal in a small-ministry group. And it is the ministry group that this book is about—a small group of believers who get together to help each member move toward God's goal of Christlikeness. The group this book describes is a growth group—a group that stimulates each member to grow in the Lord and reach his fullest potential as a Christian person.

When this kind of group meets, it meets for ministry. And its result is personal, spiritual growth— a growing experience of one another as members of Christ's body and a growing sense of intimacy in personal relationship with the Lord.

Is a group necessary?

Can't Christians reach their potential without a small-group experience?

This is a deceiving question because the answer is both yes and no. We don't need formal "small groups" for growth. But we do need significant personal relationships with other believers. No one can reach his potential in Christ *alone*.

In the last hours before the Crucifixion, Jesus placed great emphasis on togetherness for his disciples (John 13–17). Over and over the themes of love and unity recur, initiated by the new commandment, *"Love one another!"*

Jesus defined the kind of love he meant quite clearly. Believers are to love "as I have loved you" (John 15:12). And Jesus' love is a total kind of love. He left the safety of heaven and entered fully into our world to share our experiences. He participated in the lives of those he loved and gave himself fully. To love "just as" Jesus loved *must* involve us deeply with other persons.

Such involvement needn't take place just in a small group, of course. But the small group has become prominent today because so many of us have not been intimately involved with others. The depersonalization of society has struck deeply into the life of the church and robbed us of our heart and our warmth. To love Jesus' way, we must truly know and really care about one another as persons.

Probably the real question is *not* "Is a small group necessary?" but rather "Will meeting with a smaller group of Christians help me develop closer Christian relationships and help me grow toward Christlikeness?"

And that is a question each of us must answer for himself. One way to answer it is to check out what the

The Relationship

My Present Experience

	Satisfactory	?	Unsatisfactory

1. Receiving (Rom. 14:1)
   I know others who accept and value me as I am.

2. "
   I freely accept and appreciate others, even when they seem "different" from me.

3. Provoke (encourage) (Heb. 10:24)
   I have friends who encourage and stimulate me to keep on growing when I feel low.

4. "
   I am being used to motivate others to fresh trust when they are discouraged.

5. Forgive (Eph. 4:32)
   I freely confess faults to others.

6. "
   I've found freedom to forgive others.

7. "
   I am close to others who do ask forgiveness when they hurt me.

8. Bear burdens (Gal. 6:1)
   I am praying for burdens others have shared with me.

9. "
   I have recently shared my burdens and know others are praying for me.

0. Impact
   I have a warm feeling that I'm not alone in the Christian life—I'm experiencing what it means to be one of many brothers.

Bible tells us about the relationships that are to exist between Christians. If you or I already have these kinds of relationships with others now, the chances are we may *not* need a small group. If we aren't experiencing these kinds of relationships, the right kind of small group will probably make a significant contribution to our personal, spiritual growth and to the meaningfulness of our Christian life.

This chart identifies some aspects of Christian interpersonal relationships that the Bible says are important for spiritual health. These relationships, again, do not *have* to happen just in a small group, but they *do have to happen!* As the writer of Hebrews says, Christians really need to get together for ministry. "And let us consider how we may spur one another on toward love and good deeds. Let us not give up meeting together, as some are in the habit of doing, but let us encourage one another—and all the more as you see the Day approaching" (Heb. 10:24–25).

God knows we do need each other. And God has given us each other.

We *do* need to draw near.

Small groups

Many questions are raised about how to structure small Christian groups that meet together. While important, most of the questions asked are not *critical* to small-group success. But before describing what *is* critical, let me share brief answers to the questions most commonly asked.

How large should a small group be? The size varies. I've found eight or more people to be a good starting size. Most dynamic groups will grow as the group climate is established. When you get near the twenties, it's usually time to consider dividing.

At times, a very large group of hundreds will meet for part of a session and then subdivide into smaller groups for sharing and discussion. When this happens, it is important to make sure that the *same people* are in the smaller groups each time.

Where should small groups meet? You're striving for informality, for a sense of intimacy and closeness. Probably someone's home is best adapted to creating the atmosphere that helps group members open up, share, and learn to care about each other.

Should a small group be "closed" or open to anyone? Some insist that a small group be "for members only." My own experience has been that "open" groups are more dynamic. What is important is to have a highly committed core membership. Then relax and let God add those whom he wishes. Coming into a close, loving group of believers is one of the very best ways to disciple a new believer, and I've seen many non-Christians won to Christ as they were drawn by the loving concern of groups who meet for ministry.

Should a group be age-graded? I don't believe so. Our unity is not based on sociological similarity but on a shared desire to know and love Jesus better. Differences in age and experience can contribute to this goal.

How long should a small group stay together? There is really no set rule. It may be good to begin with a ten-week commitment. Then decide whether or not to go on for another three months. Most importantly, keep open to God's leading. Feel free to stop, divide, start, or to continue your small-ministry group for years.

How often should a group meet? For maximum impact, there really is no substitute for a weekly session. But many find that the press of time forces them to meet every other week instead.

Should non-Christians be invited? The group that meets for ministry is not *directly* evangelistic. Yet, I've seen many many persons become Christians through involvement in this kind of group. The key seems to be the relationship the person who comes has to the group members. It's best to invite non-Christian friends; it's least effective to invite non-Christian acquaintances. And when a non-Christian does come, he should be welcomed with the same love and warmth as a fellow believer.

What about leadership? Every group will have leaders, whether these are "officially appointed" or simply emerge. What is important is that the person who "leads" a ministry group understands his role. Such a leader is not to "control" and is not to dominate by talking constantly. Instead, the effective ministry-group leader guides and encourages sharing and often plans learning activities that will get members to look into Scripture and stimulate their participation.

How do we meet for ministry?

So far, in this introductory chapter, I've suggested that a small group that meets for ministry—to build each other up and help each other move toward God's goal of Christlikeness—can make an important contribution to any believer's life. While it is not *necessary* for Christians to be members of such a small group to have significant ministering relationships, the small group is one of the best structures to nurture such relationships.

But remember, there is no magic in "small" and no magic in "group." Just because a few people get together regularly is no guarantee that ministry will happen! That's why I had to agree with that lady from Detroit whom I mentioned at the beginning of this chapter. Many have had disappointing experiences with small groups. And usually the reason for the disappointment was first a lack of focus; second, a lack of understanding *how* to minister in the small-group setting.

This book is focused on one kind of group and one only—Christians who want to meet for mutual ministry. It is designed to help you understand what makes such a group successful and to give leaders Action Ideas for learning activities that will build those success principles into *your* group.

Part I examines five principles of group ministry. These principles suggest that for a ministry group to succeed, it needs a balance of five elements—Identification, Affirmation, Exploration, Concentration, and Adoration. Each of these is examined in a chapter of its own.

Part II contains 99 Action Ideas. And these Action Ideas are correlated with the five principles explained in the first part. In this way I hope to help you not only understand, but also begin to implement those vital processes that lead to small-group success as you meet with others for ministry.

PART I:

PRINCIPLES OF GROUP MINISTRY

MEET FOR MINISTRY

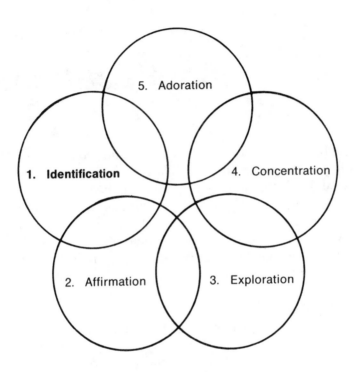

Essential Elements

1. Identification
2. Affirmation
3. Exploration
4. Concentration
5. Adoration

2

identification

Three people dropped in to tell me about a new church they had formed. They were excited about what God was doing, but troubled because of one dimension they felt had been missing. Fellowship.

Most of us feel a need for fellowship. Oh, not the superficial friendliness that sometimes passes for fellowship, but the deeper relationship that develops when Christians sense with others that somehow they are *together* in this business of living the Christian life.

The New Testament word for fellowship, *koinonia,* communicates the deepest kind of togetherness. It's a togetherness that has all things in common, that shares the most intimate experiences of life from agonies to joys. The apostle John expressed it beautifully: "We proclaim to you what we have seen and heard, so that you may also have fellowship with us. And our fellowship is with the Father and with his Son, Jesus Christ" (1 John 1:3). How exciting to realize that we never have to feel *alone* in our experience of the Christian life. God has given us others to be *with us* in a growing fellowship-relationship with Jesus.

Yet, so many Christians these days do feel alone.

They struggle to trust God more, they fail and feel guilty, and so often they never realize that others around them have the same experiences. They never realize that God has placed us together so we might support and help each other as we share experiences common to us all.

Often it is particularly hard to realize that others *are* like us; that the problems and frustrations we feel are experienced by others, too; that there is no test or temptation that has gripped us that is not "common to man"; and that God has made a way to escape so we might bear our burdens and overcome (1 Cor. 10:13). As human beings, we experience those things that *are* "common to man"—we do identify with other people. In order for us to minister to each other in a group, we must experience our identity with others.

Our identity with every man

Actually, we establish identity with other people because, first of all, we have our humanity in common.

It's important to start here. Even before a person is a Christian, there is an identity we share with him. After we come to possess God's gift of new life, we retain that identity.

Jan was brought up in a home where her father worried that she might become vain and frivolous. So he was careful to guard against any possible budding pride or apparent interest in herself. If he saw her glance in a mirror to fix her hair, he'd say, "You don't have to look in a mirror to see if you're beautiful. I'll tell you when you're beautiful." But he never told her.

Jan and her father illustrate in two ways what it means to be human beings. Jan was vulnerable; she could be hurt, and she was. Her father's approach to life crushed her and made her feel worthless and unhappy. No wonder that as an adult Jan has had a hard time accepting herself or accepting the fact that life for a Christian can be a truly new and different thing. She still hears overtones of her father's voice when she reads the Bible, and she finds it hard to believe that God is saying, "You *are* beautiful. I love you: you are fully accepted in the beloved" (see Eph. 1:6).

Jan's father? He was mistaken; he was wrong. Whatever his motives (they may have been good, or deep down there may have been a twisted motive flowing from the sin that is seated in all of our personalities), he hurt his daughter. And we're all like this. We have the capacity to hurt others. We lack the wisdom to do good, so we may be mistaken and wrong. As human beings, all of us are so limited, so far from all we want to be.

We sometimes think of "sin" only as the strong, wrong impulses that we feel. But there is far more to being a sinner than that. Biblically, sin means that our personalities are warped out of God's intended shape; that our limitations rise up and overcome us, so that even when we *want* to do good, we lack the power. As Paul says, "For what I do is not the good I want to do; no, the evil I do not want to do—this I keep on doing" (Rom. 7:19). No wonder Paul complains about "sin living in me" (v. 20).

So don't fall into the trap of thinking that people who don't know Christ are radically different from you. They're different in only one way: They lack the life of God that comes through Jesus Christ. But in their humanity, they are like you, and you are like them. In our humanity, you and I are identified with every man.

24

Establishing our human identity

It's such a peculiar thing. You and I know from our own experience how real our identity as human beings is. I know how vulnerable I am. I know how foolishly and wrongly I often act, and how easily and lightly I hurt others. I set out to do good and end up doing harm. And you know you do the same. Yet, none of us wants to admit this to others. We all want to appear strong, not weak.

Sometimes, Christians even use their faith as an excuse for failing to be honest with each other. "I'm a Christian now," we argue with ourselves. "I'm supposed to overcome these things. I'd better not let others know what I'm really like, or they won't think I'm much of a Christian!" Then, we make even Christ serve our pride.

There are several things wrong with this approach to the Christian life—several things that are destructive to our relationships with other believers.

It denies the gospel. That's right. The failure to accept and affirm our identity as human beings does deny the gospel: Jesus died for sinners (not for the "strong"). The Bible says, "when we were yet without strength, . . . Christ died for the ungodly" (Rom. 5:6, KJV). *And we never get over being the ungodly.* We never become the strong. Jesus underlines this fact when he says, "apart from me you can do nothing" (John 15:5).

The gospel is truly unique. It is God's promise to give us life and then to live that life in us. It is God's promise that when we accept our weakness and inadequacy, he will provide his supernatural power and his vitality, and he will come alive in us. *This* is the gospel. And it's such good news!

So we can see how pretending that we're strong is to deny the gospel. When we pretend to be something we aren't, we rob God of the glory that is his alone for the growth and change that is taking place in our personalities. The apostle Paul realized this, and he came to view his weaknesses (including physical disabilities) as an opportunity for God to show his power more completely. His weaknesses meant "a deeper experience of the power of Christ" (cf. 2 Cor. 12:1–11).

When I am willing to reveal my weaknesses to others, *then* they may see the power of Christ as he works in me to overcome them. Then I *demonstrate*— not deny—the gospel.

It cuts us off from others. Feeling that we have to hide our real selves from other people puts a terrible burden on us. We're forced to wear a mask all the time. The longer we try to fake it, the deeper grows the fear that sometime we'll let the mask slip. So, we tend to draw away from people because we feel uncomfortable when we come close and are vulnerable to discovery.

> Then we're truly alone.
> It's such a terrible, empty thing to be alone.
> Something inside us seems to die.

It cuts others off from help. So many Christians these days are looking for help and encouragement. They realize their inadequacies all too well and long for hope.

Bryan was a leader in his church. As a layman, he led the song services, often preached when the pastor was on vacation or out of town, and was always the first on his feet to give a testimony. He was the picture of a strong, vital, victorious Christian.

So he couldn't understand when Doug and Fran, a young couple who had recently been converted, left the church and, when asked why, cited Bryan as the reason. When he visited them, he was jolted by their explanation. "Well," Doug told him, "week after week we saw how happy you were and heard you tell of all the great things God was doing through you. But we're *not* happy. We're having an awful lot of problems being Christians. We finally decided we could just never be like you. So we quit."

Doug and Fran knew their own inadequacy too well, *and they could not identify with a person who seemed so unlike them.*

There's a biblical principle that explains what happened here and what has to happen if we are to establish identity with one another. It's found in 2 Corinthians 1, nestled in a description of God as one who

> comforts us in all our troubles, so that we can comfort those in any trouble with the comfort we ourselves have received from God. . . . If we are distressed, it is for your comfort and salvation; and if we are comforted, it is for your comfort. . . . Our hope for you is firm; because we know that just as you share in our sufferings, so also you share in our comfort.
>
> (vv. 4, 6, 7)

The apostle immediately goes on to share about "the hardships we suffered in Asia. We were under great pressure, far beyond our ability to endure, so that we despaired even of life" (2 Cor. 1:8). Paul ministered as a needy human being to other needy human beings, not as the strong to the weak.

We can see here a distinct progression of thought and experience:

—we suffer affliction
—God comforts (encourages) us
—others suffer afflictions
—we share God's comfort with them

It is because we know what it means to be human

27

and in need and because we have known the touch of God that we may bring comfort to others who will identify with us. Have you known despair? Then share it, so others may see that you are real and see in you the reality of God.

To communicate the reality of God, we must share our humanness—that inadequacy of ours that makes us need *him.*

This is what Doug and Fran struggled with. They simply could not identify with Bryan. He spoke of the great things God was doing but never shared his sense of need for God. He never revealed to them the fact that he was like them in his humanity.

A dual identity

Understanding something about identification helps us see what should be happening in a group that meets for ministry. We meet for fellowship—for the encouragement that comes when we realize that we are "in this" together with others. For this kind of fellowship, identity needs to be established on two levels.

> We need to experience our identity as inadequate and human.

> We need to experience our identity as Christ's persons, in whom Jesus lives and is working.

This is what sets the Christian apart. Not that he is "different from" others, but that while he is the same, Christ has been added! Jesus has come into the believer's personality through faith, and Jesus himself lives in him. Figure 1 shows one way we may visualize the relationship between these two identities of ours.

Each Christian is a human being, bearing all the limitations of a fallen human nature. But each believer *also* has been given the gift of Christ's life. Jesus himself is with us to live out his own life through us.

28

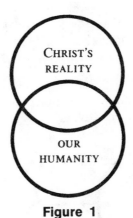

Figure 1

Our dual identity

Realistically, we can say God's goal for the Christian is that these two circles might overlap more and more. Not that we should be less human, but that Christ's adequacy might be experienced in overcoming our inadequacies. The goal of a group that meets for ministry is to encourage and stimulate this process of experiencing Christ's life!

Figure 2

Our goal: toward a
fuller experience
of Christ

To encourage movement toward this goal effectively, it is important that the members of a ministry group *establish identity with each other on both these levels!*

We need to know each other in our humanity. We need to know each other as persons in whom Jesus lives.

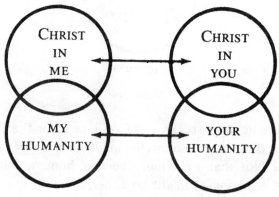

Figure 3

We need to know each other in both identities

Why some groups fail

The principle I've just stated—"Members of a ministry group need to establish identity with each other on both levels"—is a vital one. It helps us understand why some groups have been deeply disappointing to their members.

(1) *Facades.* Sometimes groups form to "study the Bible" but talk about it only in generalities or as ideas. The people in these groups fail to share on *either* level. Any hurts they feel are bottled up inside and continue to ache. Any exciting touches of God's hand are held back because sharing

them might seem to be pride. In this setting, no fellowship is experienced, and the members' lives generally remain untouched.

(2) *Phonies.* Sometimes groups develop the habit of sharing only the positive experiences: "I witnessed to three people this week"; "The Lord answered our prayers for the fourth week in a row!"; "I've felt so *good* all week." When this pattern is established, some who may have deep needs, or even passing problems, hesitate to share them. The others seem so strong there is the fear they might not understand or the fear that the others would look down on them as "less spiritual." This pattern denies the fact that we are human beings and that we are all subject to failure, frustration, pressures, and sins. Over a period of time, as our humanness is increasingly hidden, the group experience becomes more and more unreal. The phoniness and hypocrisy of the members destroy relationships, and the group dies.

(3) *Failures.* Other groups begin by exploring their needs and problems in depth. These groups may very quickly establish a sense of identity as human beings, and they often develop a healthy openness and honesty. But it is easy for such groups to limit sharing to the problem or failure level. At first, in such a group, there is a sense of release and progress. Just finding others with whom to share brings a sense of relief. But over a period of weeks or months, the feeling of progress fades, and each meeting the same old problems are hashed over again and again. Lu and Carl had another fight, so we go over their grievances again and probe and question and try to provide insight and advice. But we know that soon they'll fight again, and we'll talk it all over again. There's no *change* taking place in the

group members. Once this climate is established, such a group will often resist attempts to move toward the level of seeking identification as people in whom Christ lives. They have been trapped in a static relationship.

Static and dynamic

The group that meets for ministry seeks a dynamic experience of Jesus Christ. It's important to realize that while we must establish our identity as human beings with other members of the group, the primary reason for establishing identity on this level is to enable us to see the reality of Christ at work in our personalities.

If we can establish identity only on the human level, we set up a static situation that is destined to disappoint. *We cannot grow out of ourselves as human beings.* We change only as we release more of ourselves to Christ's control, as we learn to trust ourselves more fully to him.

Our goal, then, is to come to know each other and experience our identity both as human beings and as persons in whom Christ is a living reality. We want to see each other in our inadequacies, so we might see Christ at work in us. We share our needs and our problems, but we never *stop* there (in a static relationship). We go on to share how we are experiencing Jesus Christ in our lives. It is Christ who provides the dynamic for the small group. Seeing Jesus in others, we find hope and are freed to trust him more.

When we have this kind of relationship with other Christians, our fellowship with Christ grows too. The Bible tells us that the Holy Spirit works through members of the body of Christ to build up each individual part (Eph. 4:11–13).

32

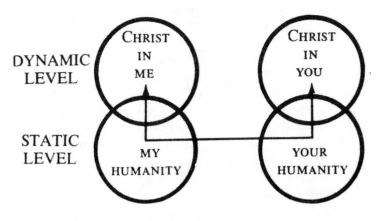

DYNAMIC
LEVEL

CHRIST
IN
ME

CHRIST
IN
YOU

STATIC
LEVEL

MY
HUMANITY

YOUR
HUMANITY

Figure 4

To establish our identity with
others, we need to see them
first as human beings, that we
might then see them as persons
in whom Christ is a living reality.

Where there is *this kind of fellowship*, growth *will* take place.

The role of the model

Why does it work this way? Why do we need each other? The only answer we can give is, really, God planned it thus. He formed us into one body; he made us brothers and sisters with a need for a family relationship. He gave each of us spiritual gifts to use in ministering to each other.

Particularly, God created us in such a way that we need models. We need to *see* in an example the reality of his words. We see this thought reflected throughout the Bible. "Let me be your example in this," Paul says a number of times. And to one church, "whatever you have learned or received or heard from me, or seen in me—put into practice. And the God of peace will be with you'' (Phil. 4:9). To Timothy he recalls the years together and the fact that the young man has thoroughly known both his teachings and his manner of life (2 Tim. 3:10); he warns Timothy to pay attention to his life and his teaching.

When elders are to be chosen, the church is told to select men whose lives exemplify the working of God in them. Peter reminds his fellow elders that they are not to act like little tin gods, but to serve as examples for the flock (1 Peter 5:1–5).

Similarly, in the Old Testament, how significant it is that parents are told first to have God's words in their own hearts and then to teach them diligently to their children (Deut. 6:1–6). Children need to see in their parents' lives the reality of the words their parents speak.

And finally, of course, there is God's own example. When it came time to communicate himself fully, he did it in a flesh-and-blood way. He became a man. In the person of Jesus Christ, we may *see* the Father.

Each of us needs models.

Each of us needs to see the reality in others' lives.

The small town where I'm from in Michigan sprawls out around a little lake. In the fall when it freezes over, you can always see along the shoreline broken limbs and rocks that have been thrown out onto the ice and have broken through. Kids like me did it— youngsters who went down to the lake when it began to freeze and wanted to see if the ice was safe for skating. We would find something heavy to throw out first to see if the ice would break.

Just imagine you're standing there now, looking out on the ice, wondering. Along comes someone else. He's read the temperatures down at the bank on Main Street, and he's sure it's safe. So he tells you, "Go on out. It's safe. I know it's safe."

34

But still you hesitate. Maybe you put your foot out tentatively and pull back as you hear the creak and moan that always marks the early ice along a shore. He's told you it's safe, but you hesitate.

Now imagine that your friend, carrying his skates, walks out onto the ice right in front of you. Turning, he looks back at you and smiles. "Come on out. See? It's safe. It holds me!"

This is what we're looking for, and what we can find, in a fellowship of believers who meet for ministry. How rich an encouragement it is when we know others *like us* who have stopped telling us to go, but who step out in front, inviting us to *come*.

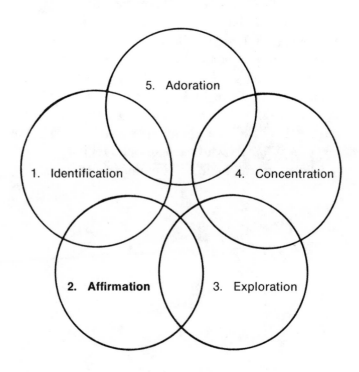

Essential Elements

1. Identification
2. Affirmation
3. Exploration
4. Concentration
5. Adoration

3

affirmation

Mal is the youngest member of a small group, which began meeting recently. At the first meeting, all the members graphed their lives to date (see Action Idea 9, p. 112), and Mal was the second to share. His story was unique, yet all too common.

Mal was born totally deaf. For eight years he could neither hear nor speak. Then he was fitted with hearing aids, and it was at this point that his life really began. He went to school and though learning was a problem, he did learn. He finished high school and went on to college. There he became a Christian, and in the early months of his life in Christ, his life peaked. He had been lonely before, uncertain in his relationships with others.

Now Mal threw himself into Campus Crusade evangelism and saw others profess Christ through his witness. He studied the Bible for hours, struggling with still nagging intellectual questions. But, despite all his activities, Mal still felt lonely. He looked at other Christians who seemed to be experiencing such abundance in their lives; he compared the emptiness he felt, emptiness that no amount of activity seemed to fill. His life seemed to drop steeply from the peaks to a dreadful, deep valley.

As Mal shared with the group his purpose for coming, he said simply that he wanted to see God's Word come alive as a reality to him, instead of an intellectual exercise. He couldn't understand why he was still lonely, why he couldn't seem to find a job, why all his time spent in Bible study and witnessing didn't deserve better results than he seemed to get from God.

A unique experience? Yes, in many ways. How few of us are born deaf and live with deficient communication for nearly a decade of our lives! How few of us have such a traumatic adjustment in trying to learn to relate to other people!

And yet, as Mal shared, it became clear that in so many ways he was just like the rest of us. So many of us have thrown ourselves into service as a way to prove to ourselves that we really are worthwhile. So many have looked at others and wondered why things seem to go so well for them and not for us. So many have felt and do feel loneliness and doubt.

As the group talked on that evening, one of the members put his hand on Mal's arm and said, "Mal, I hope one thing that comes to you through our meeting together is the awareness that God loves *you*—that *you* are important to him, totally apart from what you can do for him." Mal smiled and said, "I know what you mean. I was talking to our pastor this morning, and that's what he said I needed too. Just to realize that God really loves me."

To realize

It's so hard for many of us. Larry was in a group studying Genesis 2 and looking at all the ways God showed Adam he was important to him. As the group talked about what it means to be made "in the image of God" (Gen. 1:26, 27), Larry said it made him feel

38

frightened and uneasy. "It's such a responsibility. There are such high standards I have to live up to if I'm supposed to be like him. I don't feel comfortable with the idea at all!"

Was Larry's reaction understandable? It was totally understandable from a person who had not fully realized that God loves us *as we are* (Rom. 5:8) and that each person is valuable and important to him.

This is hard for many of us to accept.

Me?

Important to God?

Valuable?

Worthwhile?

Am I worth loving *as I am?* How can I be when all my experiences have shown me that others value me for what I do? My parents show they love me when I do what they expect. People at church accept me only when I live up to their standards. People I work with like me only when I fit in. My employer values me only when I do my job. When our experiences of life are like this, how can *we* be worth loving? How can we be worth loving when we have to struggle so hard to be accepted and when we feel so guilty and ashamed at falling short?

How can we be worth loving when we *do* fall short over and over again in marriage, in parenthood, in our neighborhood, in our work, in our struggles to become the kind of person we really want to be? How can we be worth loving *as we are?*

Feelings like these, common to Mal and Larry alike, keep us from accepting the fact that God does love and value us. Feelings like these keep us from finding the freedom both to love ourselves and to love him.

Psychologists have a term for a person who feels unhappy about himself. They say he has a "low self-image.'' Somehow he can't bring himself to accept or to like himself. And they also point out that a low self-image tends to dominate and determine a person's responses to life. A person will act in a way consistent with his picture of himself.

Carol has learned to view herself as fat and weak. When she starts one of her many new diets, she starts almost in despair. She'll try it, but she sees herself as a fat person, a weak person. And, sure enough, she loses control on the third day and goes over her limit. Ashamed and guilty and angry with herself, she goes on an eating binge. In self-hate she thinks, ''See? I know I'm no good! I'm just weak and fat and I'll always be fat.''

Carol acted in a way that confirmed her picture of herself. Though consciously she didn't want to, she still had to prove to herself that she really is the kind of person she thinks she is.

Some try desperately to prove they are *not* the kind of persons they think they are. This desire seems to have been partly at the root of Mal's active efforts in evangelism and Bible study: ''I'll prove I'm valuable by what I do. I'll show myself I'm worth loving by accomplishing great things.''

But even accomplishing much—Mal probably won more people to Christ at twenty-six than you or I ever will—didn't meet his deepest needs. He still felt alone. He still felt unloved and unlovely. Mal still couldn't accept himself *as he was*.

Who are we?

This is a basic question each of us has to answer. Who am I? *Am* I important? Is my picture of myself and my evaluation of my worth an accurate one? Or am I living in a world of illusion?

It is here that God speaks to us with a striking

message Bible-believing Christians often overlook and sometimes distort. *Each person is important.*

We hear the message first in creation. After God made all things and looked at each day's work and pronounced it "good," he made man. Genesis says something about the creation of man that is said of no other living thing. "Let us make man in our image," God said, "after our likeness; and let them have dominion over the fish of the sea, and over the fowl of the air, and over the cattle, and over all the earth, and over every creeping thing that creeps upon the earth. So God created man in his own image, in the image of God he created him, male and female he created them" (Gen. 1:26, 27, RSV).

God made man in his likeness.

Man alone.

So man is special.

And looking over that day's work, the Bible records God's evaluation: "It was *very* good" (1:31).

An objection is often raised at this point. Yes, Adam was "in God's image," but then sin entered. Man is to be seen now as a sinner. *Our awareness of ourselves as sinful is to dominate our self-image!* The "likeness" has been lost!

But has it? There are answers to this objection.

(1) Men still bear the "image of God." Genesis 9:6 gives as a reason for capital punishment of a murderer the fact that God made man in his image. Man's specialness is so significant that even in a society of sinners it must be affirmed in the most jolting way. One who dares to strike down a human being—a person who is created special to God—must himself be struck down. And so God affirms the value of even fallen, sinful man.

This same thought is repeated in James 3:9, which plainly states that men "have been made in God's likeness." Sin has distorted humanity from the pattern of the original creation and has marred the image, but the image is not lost. Each person is still special to God; each person still bears the likeness of the Eternal.

(2) "Image of God" is not, as some have thought, a synonym for holy. Holiness is one of the characteristics of God, yes. But he is a holy *person*. It is the fact that God is personal—with all the capacities of a person for knowing and feeling and valuing and interacting and doing—that is central to our image of God. In the fact that human beings are also persons, they are set apart from all the rest of creation. We are like God in our personhood.

Our characteristics differ, it is true. He is holy; we are not. He is love, and we can love but we can also be mean and spiteful. And yet, in the fact of being persons, we are like him because we're persons, we're special. He made us special, and we remain special to him.

We hear the same message in the Law. The message of the Bible that human beings are special and valued by God is, surprisingly, heard in the giving of the Law as well as in the Creation. So many with a low self-image hear the standards of God as crushing and condemning, since they view standards as responsibilities they should live up to but cannot. How exciting to realize that, while the Law is meant to crush the individual who tries to be good enough to earn God's favor (Rom. 3:19, 20), the giving of Law was an act of love. It affirmed man's specialness and value.

As Deuteronomy says, "The Lord commanded us to do all these statutes . . . for our good always" (6:24, KJV). The Law was not meant to be a way for the believer to "earn points" with God! The Law was given as an expression of love, to help the believer live a happy, meaningful life—a life that is always in touch with reality, leading to ever fuller experiences of the love of God.

In giving standards, God was not shouting demands but showing us once again, "You are special to me."

We see the message most clearly in Christ. It is in Jesus that we encounter the depths of God's love for us. How important are we? How valuable? The gospel answer is clear: *"You are important enough for me to die for!"*

When we hear this message, we simply have to stop and wonder. God knows our every inadequacy. He knows the sin that has woven tangled webs throughout our personalities. He knows the way we fail. He knows the lies we tell him, and ourselves, to try to hide our motives. He knows us as we really are.

And still he loves us.

He did not spare his own Son, but gave him up for us all . . . (Rom. 8:32).

Am I valuable?

Am I worthwhile? As I am?

Every word and every act of God in Jesus Christ says, *"Yes!* You are special to me!"

Special enough for God to give his very best.

So, it's here that we gain perspective on the balance we must strike between seeing ourselves as sinners and seeing ourselves in our essential worthwhileness and value. The fact that I am a sinner is not my *primary* identity; the fact that I am a human being is my primary identity. As a human being, I am created in the image of God, the object of the love of God, my worth measured only by the value that can be set on the death of the only Son of God. *I am loved. As I am.*

The fact that I am a sinner is a part of my *secondary* identity. It is not *essential* to who I am because through the death of Christ, sin has been dealt with. I will not always be a sinner! Christ's death stripped away that fixedness and, while he is even now untangling the webs that block me from becoming all I can be in him, I look forward to an eternity of total freedom from sin. And when sin is stripped completely away? I will still be me! A person. An individual. The *same* person. I will still be a unique human being whom God loved so much that he was willing to die to free me from something that doesn't have to be.

So you and I need to learn to see ourselves as God sees us. We need to distinguish between our primary identity (that which we are now and always will be— individuals created in the image of God and thus intrinsically valuable) and our secondary identity (that which has become a part of us—a part that Christ's cross has destroyed and his life is even now ushering out of our lives). When we learn how important we are to God, then we may begin to be important to ourselves. When we see how much God loves us, then we can begin to realize that we are actually to love ourselves!

Affirmation

Affirmation is what happens when you and I see each other as valuable and worthwhile and when we communicate this perception to each other.

Affirmation is simply communicating to another person, "You are important. You are loved."

Terri was in a small group of women who met Thursday mornings for ten weeks. It was an exciting experience! Each week the women studied and paraphrased a passage of Scripture, and then looked for ways to apply it. They told what they had been discovering and how they had responded to the Word during the week. Each prayed daily for all the others, focusing on a specific prayer request each presented weekly. And they saw their prayers being answered! There was such a sense of reality, of vitality that each felt free to express her needs and her problems, to be real with each other. And each person knew she was loved and accepted by the others.

Later another group formed. There was the same number of women—ten. They met for the same length of time. But these women were afraid to share. They talked about the Bible but hid their lives. Telling about it, Terri commented, "There never was such a bunch of women with perfect marriages, wonderful children, and absolutely joyous Christian lives, with nothing that needed being prayed for. And there never was a more meaningless group!"

Terri meant, of course, that she was experiencing a phony group (p. 31). Here were women who would not reveal their humanity, so they never came to see the reality of Jesus working in their lives.

Such groups happen, and they are most likely to happen when their members fail to realize that they can be loved *as they are*. They hide their real selves because they can't bring themselves to agree with God that they are valuable and worthwhile apart from anything they do.

Mal was this way. He had to try to do things to gain a sense of worth in accomplishment.

But this approach to life is tragically self-defeating. When we hide our real selves from others, we cut ourselves off from the fellowship we need to grow as Christians and as persons. When we try to earn God's approval, we put our relationship with him on a works basis and cut ourselves off from the experience of his presence and power (Gal. 5:4). What each of us needs to learn is that we are to accept ourselves as we are, realize that God loves us *now,* and simply open up our lives to him, to do in us what he wills.

But how do we learn to accept and love ourselves? How do we develop a better self-image?

We know we weren't born with an image of ourselves as "good" or "bad," as "valuable" or "worthless." This image developed over the years of our growing up, and it developed as we discovered how others saw us. If we had parents like those of Jan (p. 23), the chances are we began to question our worth and value. Their attempts to keep us from being proud and self-confident succeeded only too well!

Sometimes a child may have parents who set unreasonably high expectations for him to fulfill. A dad who made Phi Beta Kappa insists his son try to match his grades. An athletic older brother sets standards a younger, less-talented boy feels he has to live up to but never can. A mother whose singing career is cut short by marriage wants her daughter to sing concert music, even though she simply doesn't have the voice. A girl who is plain wants desperately to be like her attractive big sister. Often when such a child doesn't measure up, he feels it's his fault. That somehow, if he were only *better,* he'd be able to please Mom or Dad or himself. And so he, too, begins to doubt his worth and value.

We may say to such a person, "Listen! That image of yourself that's developed over the years . . . that's not the real *you.* You're not worthless! You're really important, someone worth loving." We may even say this on the authority of Scripture: "God loves you. *That's* how important you are!"

But the words alone simply do not change something that took root over so many, many years of experiences with people.

Can our self-image be changed? Really, it takes the

46

power of God, working his own supernatural transformation by the Holy Spirit. But you and I may be used by God in another person's life as a channel through which the Spirit moves! An important element of the life of a group that meets for ministry is to be so used in each other's lives. One of the most important things we may do is to affirm one another—to say and demonstrate to each other that we are loved as we are.

As a person experiences being loved and valued, God brings the truth of his words to life and that person can change.

In our small groups, we can come to know each other as we are and, knowing each other this way, show compellingly that, *as we are,* we are loved and valued.

Communicating love

The Bible gives us deep insights into how we may communicate this kind of love and valuing that we call affirmation. We see the importance of affirming in Jesus' "new" command: "A new commandment I give you: Love one another; as I have loved you, so you must love one another" (John 13:34). *Just as* Jesus loves, he values us for who we are—human beings, special to God—not for what we do.

A look at the New Testament contexts in which relationships between "one another" are described gives us insight into how to express and communicate this kind of affirming love.

"Welcome one another" (Rom. 15:7, RSV). Recently a couple told me of their experience in a local church in Phoenix, Arizona. They were struck by the friendliness the first day they visited: Several couples came up, introduced themselves, and said how glad they were to see the new folks. So the couple

returned, and again they were met by other couples and welcomed warmly. But after six weeks, they suddenly realized that while people kept saying hello, they didn't *know* anyone there. And when they realized that all the people who had been so eager to meet them were "greeters" *assigned* to be friendly that day, they felt betrayed!

This isn't what the word translated "welcome" means. It is a far more significant word—one implying both "accept" and "welcome into close relationship." And how complete our acceptance is to be! Romans 14:1 uses the same term, and says, "Accept him whose faith is weak, without passing judgment on disputable matters." Don't even try to change his views! Welcome him as someone who is *important for himself.*

How do we communicate to a person that he is accepted and welcomed into fellowship? Several ways. (1) We listen to him. In listening we show him that his feelings, experiences, and ideas are important to us: *He* is important. (2) We share with him. We open our lives to him and in sharing invite him to come closer to us as persons—the kind of invitation we give only to people we consider important. (3) We resist the temptation to try to "convert" him. All of us have been in situations where the price of acceptance was *agreeing.* We must resist seeming to want to change a person, even when he's wrong. How can we? We must remember that God is the only one who can work real changes in a person's heart. Our attempts to convince will only communicate to another person that we have put a price on our acceptance, whether we actually have or not! No wonder the Word commands, "Welcome him but not for disputes over opinions!"

"Carry each other's burdens" (Gal. 6:2). This, too,

is a unique way to show love and acceptance in an interaction of expressed concern.

Sometimes we think this verse implies only that we listen to another person's problems and then promise to pray for him or help him. But it means far more. It means that each of us needs to *bare* our burdens as well as bear them!

How does this affirm another person? When we simply listen to *his* needs and show concern, we are actually implying a superior-inferior relationship. We're communicating a sense of being above him and we may be sure that this will only confirm another's low estimate of himself! But when we open ourselves to be *ministered to,* we communicate something else entirely. We show that we value the other person and his ministry. We demonstrate, and thus affirm, that he seems important to us.

Strikingly, when the ministry of bearing burdens is a mutual one—a bearing of *one another's* burdens—then neither person involved comes to see himself as "higher" than another. Instead, each lifts the other up to a higher level *with him!* In bearing one another's burdens, we constantly affirm the value and worth of each other and agree with God that we *are* important. We are worthy of being loved.

"Let us consider one another to provoke unto love . . ." (Heb. 10:24, KJV). The Revised Standard Version accurately translates the archaic "provoke" into "let us consider how to stir up one another to love and good works."

This is a ministry of affirming one another by showing both trust and expectation. As Christians, we may *expect* God to be working in us. We may expect him to be working through us. We may expect him to be changing us. Because Christ is in us, the Bible says, we have hope for all the glorious things that are to come (cf. Col. 1:27). So we can encourage and stir up each other to act in the faith and confidence that God will act in us!

This is entirely different from struggling to do something we know we can't do because we are so weak and impotent, or from trying to prove our value by our accomplishments. This is affirming that in Christ our potential as persons may be realized. *He* is able. Now we can see each other in positive ways. We do not need to live defeated lives or mourn together about our failures. We are so valuable and important to God that he has acted in Christ to free us and to enable us.

How encouraging it is to realize that other Christians think of me now, not as unable, but as enabled! So, by encouraging and expecting each other to act in our newness (yet accepting one another in our humanity should we fail), we testify to each other that the old images of ourselves are wrong. They may be joyfully discarded!

There are others. Ministries that seem on the surface even to be negative—like reproving or rebuking—prove on examination to be affirming. Yet, it often is so hard to "speak the truth in love" when we are afraid the truth might hurt or embarrass.

But see what we communicate about the other person when we hold back! We are saying that we don't trust him, that we are afraid he'll take what we say wrongly, that he is such a weak person he will be unable to bear the truth, or that he is just not important enough for us to run the risk of possible interpersonal discomfort! Yet when something is blocking a relationship, when there is something that needs to be said and is held back, the barrier is always sensed. And it is always read, and rightly so, as failure to trust the other person.

Now, this is not to encourage blunt or attacking criticism. This is saying that the truth is to be spoken *in love*. When even a negative truth (a rebuke, or reproof) is spoken in love, it becomes an affirmation of the value of the other person to us and an affirmation of our respect for him.

So also are all the "one another" ways of living together recorded in Scripture. When we learn to live with each other in an affirming, loving fellowship, we release one another from so much that blocks the free working of the Holy Spirit in our hearts and lives.

This, then, is the second element in the life of the group that meets for ministry. We meet to help each other realize who we really are as persons of worth and value, persons who are the object of God's love, persons who can come to accept and love themselves because we *are* loved.

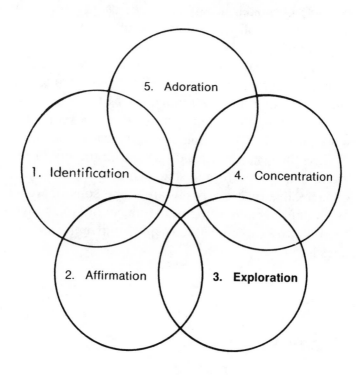

Essential Elements

1. Identification
2. Affirmation
3. Exploration
4. Concentration
5. Adoration

4

exploration

Some of my driest times spiritually came while I was in seminary, studying the Bible every day. I know it's not supposed to be that way. But it was, for me and for many others.

After all, there's nothing magical about the Bible. A chapter a day doesn't keep the doldrums away. Hours in and out of the classroom getting to know a lot about Scripture won't work like Alice's magic mushroom land to transform you into a spiritual giant. Yet, the Bible is very important to the health of the group that meets together for ministry.

Discovering God's point of view through Scripture is important for every Christian, *but not as an end in itself.* Getting into the Bible together is important as a means—a means that God uses to bring our lives, thoughts, and actions into harmony with him and each other. The Bible is a means he uses to transform us and our experiences.

It's with this realization that we need to approach God's Word in our small groups. The Bible is not just for learning, but for living.

Illusion and reality

We desperately need Scripture to guide us in our living.

The reason for this is simple. Reality is so often hidden from us. The appearances of things around us deceive. Illusions masquerade and blind our senses so that what we perceive as true, as real, as helpful is often utterly false.

For instance, a "crusading psychologist," Dr. Robert L. Wolk, published a book entitled *The Right to Lie*.* His thesis is that if children are taught to tell lies, when they do lie they'll avoid "ego-damaging guilt"; thus, in various situations lying is the best way possible to show love. If youngsters learn to use lies considerately and appropriately, they will be better able to "cope with the demands of reality."

But do we know reality? Will a lie really preserve us from harm or show love for others? Is life something to manipulate with lies? Or is the idea that lies can make a positive contribution to the happiness of others merely an illusion—a shadow cast by a sin-warped perception of life? How do we know what life is *really* like?

The Bible hints that one of the links in the chain binding us to our humanity is the fact that we are blind to reality. We're blind, but we think we see. In Ephesians, Paul calls this distorted idea of life "the ways of the world" (2:2). John speaks bluntly of walking in light and darkness. He warns that if we deny revealed reality, "we deceive ourselves and the truth is not in us" (1 John 1:8).

Throughout the Bible, "truth" and "reality" display an intimate connection. "Truth" in Old and New Testaments, in the original languages, implies the concept of "light; in him there is no darkness at all." We see this connection clearly in the 1 John passage (vv. 5–10).

*Robert L. Wolk and Arthur Henley, *The Right to Lie: A Psychological Guide to the Uses of Deceit in Everyday Life* (New York: Peter H. Wyden, 1970). p. 78

Here God is presented as light, with no shadow of darkness existing in him. To enjoy fellowship with him, the believer cannot go on "living in darkness." To claim fellowship with such a God while we live in darkness, "we lie and do not live by the truth" (v. 6).

But what is "darkness"? Is it sin? No, it's not! Even in fellowship, John says, we must still rely on the blood of Christ to keep on cleansing us from all sin. John's talk of light and dark is not of sin, *but of reality!* "If we claim to be without sin," he says (v. 8), we live in that world of illusion and lose contact with truth. We must come to see ourselves as we are and honestly face our helplessness and inadequacy. Failing to face the fact of sin keeps us struggling to perform. "If we confess our sins," the Word continues, "he is faithful and just and will forgive us our sins and purify us from all unrighteousness. If we claim we have not sinned, we make him out to be a liar and his word has no place in our lives" (1 John 1:8–10).

"Darkness," then, speaks of *denial of God's diagnosis* and *failure to live in harmony with it!* "Light," on the other hand, speaks of reality as it is known and revealed by God. So, to know reality as God knows it, to respond to life guided by his perceptions of what is real, is walking in the light.

This is what Bible study is all about! We study the Bible to distinguish reality from illusion, and we stake our lives on the trustworthiness of God's revelation by determining to *live* by the Word.

A basic choice

This is a basic choice the Christian has to make and stand by.

And it's so reasonable. God alone has a vantage point from which to see reality. He alone is able to diagnose, to share an accurate perception of reality with us. He alone knows the truth.

But in the Scripture he has revealed it.

Sometimes people make a distinction between Scripture as a "relational" book and a book of "objective" or "propositional" truth. The two ideas, though, are not to be seen in *contrast,* but in their relationship to each other. God's Word *is* relational truth: Every expression of the Word is to be read through Christ, and every expression shows us how to live in harmonious relationship with God or ourselves or others or our universe. But it is because God's Word is true—reality communicated into us as true information—that the relationships we may experience through the Word are possible. Unless we want to lose ourselves in darkness, we must accept the diagnosis of God's Word, accept the reality revealed, and pattern our lives fully on his truth.

So, we have to choose.

And the choice we must make, and help each other hold firmly to as we meet for ministry, is to *do* the Word of God.

A burden?

There's something both safe and harmless in a Bible that we meet to debate over. If the Bible is just information, merely ideas to hold detached discussions about, then we need feel no compulsion to change or to act. But when we see Scripture as truth and light, something to illuminate life and show us how to live it, we develop a deep sense of burden.

Life is difficult enough as it is. If there is *more* we are supposed to do and to be, how do we bear it?

But when we understand the full implications of what it means to say, "The Bible reveals reality," even that burden is removed! We no longer have to hear the words of Scripture as a demand. We may hear them as *an invitation to experience reality.*

Some time ago I read a book about prayer that terrorized me. It took a number of familiar verses and constructed a set of "seven conditions" for getting answers. If these conditions were fulfilled, the author said, prayer would be answered. Otherwise, we had little hope.

The idea disturbed me, but as I read verse after verse, I became convinced. The Bible *did* teach "conditions" for answered prayer! I could see no way out.

—"When you pray in faith, believing, you shall receive."

—"When you ask anything in God's will."

And my heart sank. I knew my prayers more often expressed hesitation than faith. I knew that often I was uncertain about his will. And I felt trapped, cut off from God by obstacles I couldn't overcome.

Then I learned to see the Word of God as reality, and everything changed. The "conditions" took on new form, and I learned something of the differences between "if" and "then."

What differences? Let's see by looking at two situations. (1) A mother is watching TV. Her son comes in the door, and without taking her eyes off the set, she warns him, "If you walk in front of me and block my view, I'll club you!" A conditional statement has been made. (2) Another mother is cooking dinner when her son comes in. She sees him look inquiringly toward the stove and warns, "If you touch that pot, you'll get burned." Again, a conditional statement has been made, but what a difference!

The first statement we must regard as a selfish demand, a coercive attempt to force the child to the mother's will. The second we regard as love. There's no coercion here, and it is clearly the child's safety the mother considers. The harm arises from the natural consequences of disregarding the reality of the hotness of the pot—a reality the child was made aware of by the mother's statement. Both mothers' statements are conditional, *but the motive and tone of voice and what is being communicated make them entirely different!*

It's the same with the Bible. Is God shouting conditions and demands, like the first mother did, and warning us of dire consequences if we dare displease him? Or is our God like the second mother, enlightening, loving, opening up the possibility of new ways to live by showing us the reality of what will harm us and what will help? We have no doubts that God *loves* us. His every word is spoken in the honest tones of love.

How, then, am I to understand the "conditions" associated with prayer? As the promise of a reality that in Christ I may pray in faith, believing. To do so is a reality that I may experience, and in experiencing, *know* that my prayer is being answered. To know his will is a possibility, and this, too, I may experience. I am invited to experience more reality in prayer than I have.

God is not shouting his demands at me.

God is inviting me closer, showing me what blessings he has in store!

But what of our humanness?

To realize that the Bible is God's portrait of reality and his invitation to experience reality helps us throw off the guilt and shame that grip us when we feel, "I ought . . ." God's Word does not pile burdens on us; it opens doors!

Here I'm again struck by my humanness. I catch a fresh awareness of my inability even to accept his invitation. *The Bible may describe reality, but where do I go for power to experience it?*

Here there's a third dimension of Bible study, one that completes and vitalizes the first two. Remember, we've seen so far that

—the Bible is for living (not just for learning).

—the Bible reveals a reality we are to experience. But whenever we *try* to experience what Scripture speaks of, we discover again how human and weak we are. *How* do I approach Scripture to find it becoming true in me?

The answer God gives us is very simple.

We approach the Bible in faith.

With confidence.

Too often we approach living by the Scriptures by making an "honest effort" or "trying." This is how many believers describe their Christian lives. But the very words reveal a tragic misconception—a retreat in relationship with God from a grace to a performance (or works) basis.

It's hard to grasp, but perhaps we can see that even to speak of faith as "trying" turns attention to ourselves. It assumes, to some extent at least, that *we,* not Christ, are responsible for our lives. When we turn back to ourselves for resources to experience God's reality, we find ourselves trapped in the impotence of our humanity.

The same Bible that reveals reality teaches us to cast off *all* thought of performance and fixes our attention on Christ. Peter walked safely on the waves as long as his gaze was fixed on the Lord but he sank when that gaze was distracted. We, too, are invited by the Word to keep our eyes on Christ; we are told that God's plan is to *impart* righteousness, not demand it. And this, the Bible says, is a process begun and continued by faith. So, the Scripture reminds, "the righteous will live by faith" (Rom. 1:17).

Some time ago, my children had a peculiar game. It consisted of some clear plastic over a cardboard square, enclosing metallic dust and a magnet. For hours the children would sit and shape and reshape that dust with the magnet. They formed faces, little men, animals, all sorts of things. The dust responded to the magnet's pull.

Faith operates this way. It would be foolish to talk of the dust moving by "its magnetic power." The power rests in the magnet; the dust merely responds. It would be just as foolish to speak of "faith" as though it were some power in us. We respond. The power to change is God's.

So "living by faith" takes on a peculiar character. *We respond to God's Word as to one who is utterly faithful.*

This is "the law of the Spirit of life set me free from the law of sin and death" (Rom. 8:1). *Christ lives in me.* His power frees. Turning away from every thought of strength or trying, we are free to respond to the promptings of the Spirit through his Word.

"Faith" faces the reality of who we are—the reality of humanity and our weakness. But faith responds to *do* the Word of God, expecting nothing from ourselves! Faith responds to *do* in the amazing conviction that *in the doing* Christ's own power and Christ's own life will actually control and enable us!

We can step out and obey the Word of God because Christ *is* in us. He brings us hope for glorious things to come.

The place of the Word

When a group meets for ministry, the Scripture must play a central role in the experience. We may summarize the particular functions of the Bible in the group meeting this way.

(1) The Bible is explored for light and truth. We know that God's revelation gives us an accurate picture of every reality we need to understand. We come to see God as he is; we come to understand ourselves; we discover how we may live to please God and experience his joy and love.

Therefore, an important part of our shared study is study itself—a serious look at the Word of God to understand what he is saying to us.

Several things will help us here. First, we're helped by an *overall grasp* of the Bible book in which we're looking. This keeps us from misunderstanding verses or paragraphs and taking them out of context.

For instance, in one place an anguished Job cries out,

> But he stands alone and who can oppose him?
> He does whatever he pleases.
> He carries out his decrees against me,
>   and many such plans he still has in store.
> This is why I am terrified before him;
>   when I think of all this, I fear him.
>
> (Job 23:13–15)

Is this an accurate picture of God? Should our thoughts and feelings about him be those of Job?

Our answer comes when we understand the development and theme of the book itself.

What Job is saying accurately expresses his feelings at the time and often may express our feelings, too. When we understand the Book of Job as the sufferer's struggle to come to grips with his experience, and when we see the end of the process in God's revelation of himself and his blessing of Job, we are able to put this anguished paragraph in perspective.

There are other Bible passages about suffering that do more than share experiences. They help us to understand God's purposes in suffering. Two of these are James 1:2–18 and Psalm 73.

Outline of Job

Passage	Development
Job 1:1–2:10	Gives the background of Job's experience: Satan's challenge to test Job—which test Job passed (cf. 1:11; 2:5, 10).
Job 2:11–31:40	Job and his three friends debate the cause of his suffering. Through several rounds of dialogue, no one can suggest any cause but sin, though Job continues to state his innocence.
Job 32:1–37:24	Elihu, an observer of the dialogue, breaks the impasse by demonstrating other purposes God may have for allowing suffering than as punishment for sin.
Job 38:1–41:34	God speaks to Job from a whirlwind and contrasts his power and wisdom with Job's limited understanding and ability.
Job 42:1–16	Job, now knowing God firsthand, submits fully to him and his purposes; all he has lost is restored double.

It's important when reading a Bible passage to jot down thoughts and insights, either before the group meets or during the group meeting. Such notes may summarize content or focus on personal application. Here are some notes that summarize content from James and some notes on Psalm 73 that record snatches of specific verses and personal-application questions jotted beside them.

James 1:2–18

— *Consider it pure joy whenever you face various trials (v. 2).*
Why?
They test faith (proving its strength) (v. 3), "road-testing" cars.
The product is steadfastness (stability) and ultimately maturity (v. 4).
(Maturity's worth a lot to me!)

— *We can expect God to give us wisdom (how-to knowledge rather than information!) when we're in a bind (v. 5), as long as we keep our trust focused on him (v. 6).*

— *The real problem with testing and temptation isn't outside; it's inside us (vv. 12–15). God doesn't put us in spots to force us to sin; wrong responses to things come from our inner desires, our inner natures. (Maybe the big problem, then, is our being upset when something unfair happens.) Back to that "joy" response again (v. 2).*

Man, that's asking a lot!

Some groups approach the Bible from the point of view of personal problems. In their sharing they discover something that troubles them, and they want answers. Recently a small group my wife and I were in saw several members uncertain about prayer. During the next weeks we each studied the Bible and then brought what we'd learned to the group meeting for discussion. In those weeks each person's nagging

Psalm 73

v. 3 I envied the arrogant when I saw the prosperity of the wicked.	Is that what's eating at us? Envy?
v. 5 They are free from the burdens common to man. . . .	Why don't they have problems like we do? They sure do seem to get away with it.
v. 10 Their people turn to them and drink up waters in abundance. . . .	Why does God let them get away with it? They do lead others to follow their example.
v. 11 They say, "How can God know?"	Is their view of God best? He sure doesn't seem to act very fast!
v. 13 Surely in vain have I kept my heart pure.	Sometimes it sure does seem a waste of time to try and do right. Why doesn't it pay off? What's the good of it, anyway?
v. 17 Till I entered the santuary of God; then I understood their destiny.	Guess we do have to evaluate in terms of eternity as well as time. How much of our upset comes from caring too much about things that aren't important?
v. 18 Surely you place them on slippery ground. . . .	Success dangerous? I never thought of it that way, but it's true. Maybe we've been getting on too well as it is. Is God reminding us of him by this trouble? Of our values?

uncertainties were settled, and we found a fresh confidence in God as real questions were answered by him.

Other groups begin with a common passage of Scripture and study it to determine just what God is showing us about reality. Either approach is suitable for a small group. But unless the Bible does have a central role in the group's experience, the group will not realize its full potential. We *are* subject to illusion. We desperately need to check our every thought and perception against the portrait of reality God has lovingly given in the Scriptures.

(2) The Bible is for living, not simply for learning. God's objective revelation of truth is always to be explored in view of its impact on human experience.

Here's where group study can make a unique contribution. When each person shares, "Here's how I see this truth affecting my life," our vision expands. The Holy Spirit works through each of us to illumine and make clear the *meaning to me* of what God has said to us all.

When group members have learned to relate openly and honestly with one another, to experience both the identification and affirmation aspects of group life, they are freed to share (and to see) what the Bible means to them.

It is vital that whenever the Bible is studied, we move together from "what is revealed" to state clearly "what this means to me."

(3) The Word is to be experienced. This last element simply means that we are to *do* what we've seen in Scripture. We are to obey, to "continue in" Christ's words, to "keep my words."

To act.

Here, too, we need to share. We may share both what we have done in obedience to the Word and what we feel God wants us to do this coming week.

This kind of sharing is important. In it we may remind each other to step out in faith because we can rely on God to make the act of obedience possible in us. We may pray for each other, a vital ministry in view of the fact that it is Jesus' supernatural power at work in us and the fact that our God answers prayer.

This sharing is particularly important as encouragement. When week after week, we see God actually working out his life in others who have responded in faith to the Word, we find our own trust in God increasing. When we see God working in others, we sense in new ways the presence the power of God has in us. Then, we're moved to praise and to trust him even more.

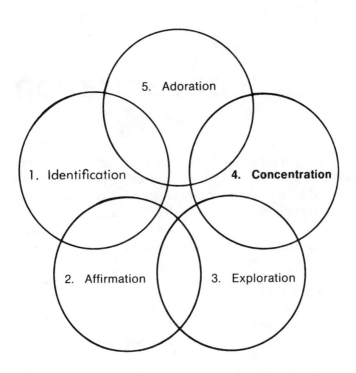

Essential Elements

1. Identification
2. Affirmation
3. Exploration
4. Concentration
5. Adoration

5

concentration

It happened again Sunday. We started our time together looking at the key verse: "All things were created by him, and for him [Jesus]" (Col. 1:16). Then I asked each person to complete the sentence: "I was made for Jesus to . . ." The adults came up with some exciting suggestions. I was made for Jesus

to trust him	to be a good steward
to worship him	to do his work
to be a good father	to be like him
to relax in him and	to enjoy life
be a channel	to thank him

It's deeply moving to realize afresh that "Christ himself is the Creator who made everything in heaven and earth, the things we can see and the things we can't" (Col. 1:16, LIVING BIBLE) and that you and I are among all that was made by him and for him! Yet, as we explored together, Dave (a newcomer to our class) commented, "I was made for Jesus to witness, and I believe that's my obligation. I'd like to think of it as a privilege, but right now I feel it is an obligation."

I was made by Jesus and for Jesus. Must the realization of who we are and who God is bring with it a feeling of burden and obligation?

Certainly, it has had this impact. In Nehemiah's day, the Jewish people were returning from exile in Babylon. Called to Jerusalem, there they heard for the first time the Word of God read and taught clearly (Neh. 8:7, 8). The Bible says, "all the people had been weeping as they listened to the words of the law" (v. 9). They were suddenly overwhelmed when they realized all they were not and all they had not done. The Word came to them; they heard it as obligation; they were crushed.

But the leaders responded, "This day is sacred to the LORD your God. Do not mourn or weep. . . . Go and enjoy choice food and sweet drinks, and send some to those who have nothing prepared. This day is sacred to our Lord. Do not grieve, for the joy of the LORD is your strength" (vv. 9, 10). Don't hear the Law only as a revelation of your weakness. This day—this day of looking into the Word—is set aside to the Lord. See him and realize that the joy of the Lord is your strength.

What a difference in these two approaches to Scripture.

The one emphasizes self as our human limitations are reflected against his standards. The other looks beyond self to see the Lord and finds in him rejoicing and strength.

Strength

We saw in an earlier chapter that sharing in a small group should take place on a dual level: the level of our humanity and the level of our experience with Jesus. The first level we called a *static* level because while we find some initial relief in sharing our needs and problems and in being accepted as we are, there is no power in this kind of relationship. This fact is verified by behavioral science research, which shows that groups begin characteristically with high levels of enthusiasm but over a period of time fail to meet expectations. Disappointment sets in.

But for the group meeting for ministry, there is a *dynamic* level of relationship that is open. On this dynamic level, significant changes *do* take place; growth and transformation occur. And the critical factor in living together on this level? *To share our experience of Jesus and to concentrate on helping each other see just who he is for us.*

We can help each other look away from ourselves and the burden of obligation. We can help each other look to Jesus and find strength through joy in him.

That is what the title of this chapter suggests. We are to accept and be ourselves with each other, to affirm and love each other, to study the Word together. But in it all, we are to concentrate on Jesus. We are to seek to grasp more and more of who he is. Paul's prayer for the Ephesians seems to sum up what we need in our ministry groups:

> . . . the eyes of your heart enlightened in order that you may know the hope to which he has called you, the riches of his glorious inheritance in the saints, and his incomparably great power for us who believe. That power is like the working of his mighty strength, which he exerted in Christ when he raised him from the dead and seated him at his right hand in the heavenly realms.

> (Eph. 1:18–20)

We are an inheritance for him, and he glories in us. His power in us is immeasurable, and we are to glory in him. When we realize who Jesus is, we are free to joy in him, and then we find the strength to grow and change.

It helps, then, to bring into focus just who Jesus is for us and to remind each other, as we read the Word and share, that it is *this Jesus*, not ourselves, not even God's standards, on whom we must concentrate.

Who is Jesus for us?

Most members in a group meeting for ministry will know Jesus as Savior. But Christ's work is not fully summed up in the redemption and forgiveness that come to us with our first faith in him. That's the beginning, yes. But he goes beyond that. He totally involves himself in our whole life and experience. He is the victor—victor over Satan, over sin, and even over the poverty and weakness of his adopted brothers.

We may see Jesus in several of these "victor" roles in Scripture.

Jesus, overcomer. The miracles of Jesus are often cited as authenticating his claim to deity. And they do this, but they do far more.

The Jews who clustered around Jesus were seeking a messiah—someone who would claim royal power and overthrow the Roman oppressors, which in that day controlled Palestine as well as most of the Western world. Yet, as Jesus continued to minister and teach, he seemed to take no steps toward assuming political power. Many were puzzled. Even his cousin John the Baptist, who had first announced him as Messiah, was uncertain. John had been jailed by Herod. Perhaps John's doubt was only the natural depression of an active man, a man with a sense of mission cut off from activity. But doubt he did. At last, he sent followers to ask Jesus if he were the one who was to come or if they should look for another. The Bible tells us what the Lord sent John's followers to report: "Go back and report to John what you see and hear: The blind receive sight, the lame walk, those who have leprosy are cured, the deaf hear, the

71

dead are raised, and the good news is preached to the poor" (Matt. 11:4, 5).

What a catalog of miracles! But more significantly, *what* miracles! Every one of the miracles Jesus mentioned is a miracle that meets the desperate needs of men and women.

If Jesus were concerned only with authenticating his claim to be Messiah, what startling things he might have done! Elijah and Elisha made fire fall from heaven—Jesus could have. Moses stretched his hand over the waters, and they opened—Jesus could have. Joshua saw the sun stand still—Jesus could have commanded, and it would have blinked out! But Jesus' miracles were those that met the needs of people. Jesus' miracles overcame human infirmities.

See what is revealed? First, that even when glorifying himself, God is deeply concerned with individuals. Second, that Jesus' limitless power is focused on one thing—overcoming the infirmities of men.

And this is the Jesus we know today! This overcomer, who focused his power to enable the unable, is our God. He is ready to do exactly this in our lives today!

Suzie and her husband are new Christians. Immediately after his conversion, John began to share Christ with the men on the job. It didn't affect his work. John's the conscientious type; overly conscientious, Suzie sometimes thinks. But John's witnessing really upset his supervisor. Finally the supervisor, by lying, got John fired. The more John thought about it, the more hurt and angry he became. Bitterness grew until suddenly John realized what was happening to his attitude. He couldn't change it or root out the hurt, so he turned it over to Jesus. And God brought him a great peace and calm.

As John shared this in church with us, he began by

thanking God for the new job he had provided in answer to our prayers. But it was clear that what meant most to him was the joy of seeing God work in his personality. To see Christ give him the freedom to forgive!

Jesus is overcomer today. What is your infirmity? Your weakness? Your need? Look to Jesus and see him focusing all the power of God to meet that need and to free you to glorify him.

Jesus, Lord. When we see Jesus, we have to be gripped by the consciousness that he is Lord. Paul, later in the Ephesians passage quoted earlier, points out that the resurrected Jesus is seated at the Father's right hand,

> far above all rule and authority, power and dominion, and every title that can be given, not only in the present age but also in the one to come. And God placed all things under his feet and appointed him to be head over everything for the church, which is his body, the fullness of him who fills everything in every way. (Eph. 1:21–23)

Jesus' lordship has a multiple impact for us. First, because Jesus is Lord we are free to accept all that God brings into our lives with joy and in peace. Jesus is "far above" *all* rule and authority. Jesus is in charge. Knowing his love for us, we may rest in the confidence that all he permits is an active gift of love for us.

Sometimes, this is hard to believe. Brad, a teen in our church, was lying near death with cancer. His mom and dad sat with him and suffered their own unique pain. Yet in the experience, seeing Jesus as Lord brought peace. Brad expressed his readiness to be with the Lord. And one night, as his mother— aching with the pain of seeing her son suffer—felt she could stand it no more, she turned to the Lord and gave Brad freely back to him. Brad was to be fully his, not hers. And then peace came.

Jesus is Lord. His rule means for us his protective care and guidance. But even when his choice involves us in some pain or suffering, we may know that he is Lord and find peace in remembering that he is also love.

Second, Jesus' lordship means that he is our Head. As our Head, Jesus directs our lives and leads us. How good to know we're not left to ourselves and our own understanding as we struggle to make our choices. We may *know* what is best through principles he shares in his Word, then through the guiding ministry of the Holy Spirit as he leads each individual into the distinctive path of life God has planned for him.

Jesus is Lord.

Seeing him as Lord, we give him full control, and we let him be Lord to us.

Jesus, indweller. A third theme we need to grasp to realize who Jesus is for us is expressed in the idea of "indwelling." Jesus is not an absentee God. He is not even merely a model—someone whom we look away to—to see what our life ought to be like. It is true that he is our example. "Follow me," Jesus said, and he implied both an imitation and a commitment to his lordship.

But Jesus makes it possible for us to follow him by being present with us! Luke opens the Book of Acts with a reminder that he has previously written a gospel to share "all that Jesus began to do and to teach" (Acts 1:1). Luke continues, reporting all that Jesus keeps on doing and teaching in the persons of believers! Jesus has not left us. Jesus is here now, *doing* in and through us.

Because Jesus lives in us, we may live in him.

Each of these portraits of Jesus helps us to concentrate on him when we explore Scripture and our lives. When we understand who Jesus is for us, then we can begin to experience his Word with joy and do that Word with strength. We can't do it ourselves. But Jesus can and will.

> Jesus is the overcomer. He will overcome our weaknesses and free us from the infirmities that keep us from growth and change.

> Jesus is Lord. He is in control of the universe and every circumstance that confronts us. He is eager to guide and to direct us as we give him control over our lives.

> Jesus is within. We can be like him, for he is within us to express his love and concern for people through us.

If we know Jesus in these ways—as overcomer, Lord, and indweller—our whole life changes. We suddenly discover that life cannot be summed up in our limitations. We *can* live beyond ourselves.

Listening for Jesus' voice

One of the most exciting of the Bible's teachings is that Jesus, our living Lord, gives us personal guidance. The one who is within us communicates his will in ways that we can sense, if not completely explain.

Hebrews speaks of a "today" voice of God, which comes to his people of every generation. Hebrews tells of the Exodus generation, the generation that lived to enter the Promised Land, the generation of David's day, and the believers of his own day. To them and to us, he says,

> Today, if you hear his voice,
> do not harden your hearts
> as you did in the rebellion,

during the time of testing in the desert.

(Heb. 3:7, 8)

Hebrews stresses remaining open to God and being willing to respond. Here, too, being a part of a ministry group can help. Hebrews goes on to say, "See to it, brothers, that none of you has a sinful, unbelieving heart that turns away from the living God. But encourage one another daily, as long as it is called today, so that none of you may be hardened by sin's deceitfulness" (Heb. 3:12–13).

In another passage Paul makes it very plain that the Holy Spirit, who gave us the words of Scripture, speaks to the believer through the Word and unveils the mind of Christ for him.

> ... we speak, not in words taught us by human wisdom but in words taught by the Spirit, expressing spiritual truths in spiritual words. The man without the Spirit does not accept the things that come from the Spirit of God, for they are foolishness to him, and he cannot understand them, because they are spiritually discerned. The spiritual man [e.g., the person in tune with the Spirit of God] makes judgments about all things, but he himself is not subject to any man's judgment:
> "For who has known the mind of the Lord that he may instruct him?"
> But we have the mind of Christ.
>
> (1 Cor. 2:13–16)

As we make Jesus the focus of our time together, remembering that he is living and that he does speak to us today, we become more and more sensitive to his will. We *do* sense the mind of Christ for us, and we experience his personal guidance in our own life as well as see him guiding our brothers and sisters.

This experience of Christ as one who provides daily guidance, who speaks to us through the Spirit and the

76

Word with a living voice, is one of the most important dimensions of our meeting for ministry.

The touch of Jesus

Many Christians find it hard to see Jesus as we've just viewed him. They're eager to sense the touch of Jesus in their lives but have settled down to live in quiet desperation, convinced against their will that there is reality for them only beyond the grave and in the resurrection.

But Jesus dealt with such concerns thoroughly in his upper room discourse, particularly in answer to a question from one of his disciples: "But, Lord, why do you intend to show yourself to us and not to the world?" (John 14:22). It was a good question, a vital one: Jesus, how do you make yourself plainly and clearly visible to your own people—without being seen by men of the world? Jesus' answer was simple, yet pointed, "If a man loves me, he will keep my word, and my Father will love him, and we will come to him and make our home with him" (v. 23).

Love produces obedience.

And in obedience the reality of God's presence is made plain.

It shouldn't be hard to understand this. Sometimes we try to obey out of a sense of duty. Then obedience is a grudging struggle, an attempt to do what we feel God demands of us. But this is always doomed to failure. We're not able to do all we should. When we approach Scripture and live with this attitude, we experience only the reality of our own inadequacy. No matter how hard we try, we fail (cf. Rom. 7:15).

But sometimes we're moved by love to obey. And what a different focus! Love doesn't think of itself; love fixes its eyes on the loved one. When this happens, we're aware of Jesus, and we discover in amazement that we have done what we could never do before! In forgetting ourselves and thinking of Jesus, we have moved from the *static* to the *dynamic* in life, and we actually experience the reality of Jesus' adequacy.

There are two realities that we may experience:

(1) The reality of our inadequacy.

(2) The reality of Jesus' adequacy.

When we concentrate on Jesus and our love for him, Jesus fulfills his promise that his disciples will "keep my words." In the actual doing of the word, which requires this divine enabling, we experience God's power. *And it is in this experience of God's power that we plainly see Jesus!*

Throughout the significant upper room chapters (John 13–17), this thought is emphasized and reemphasized. "Abide in me," Jesus encourages. "Live close to me." How? "If you obey my commands, you will remain in my love, just as I have obeyed my Father's commandments and remain in his love" (John 15:10). Staying close to Jesus involves loving him, love-motivated obedience, and the actual experience of Jesus' enabling us to live beyond ourselves.

When this is your experience and mine, we have no more questions about the reality of Jesus. We have touched him, and he has touched our lives. We have felt his presence. We *know*.

So, meeting for ministry is even more clearly seen. We meet to study the Bible, but not to find rules to keep. Not to find new doctrines or to defend our old ones. Not because knowing more about the Bible will make us better or "more spiritual." We study the Bible to see Jesus as enabler, as Lord, as present with us.

When we see him as enabler, we realize that, whatever the Word says, we need not feel crushed or under obligation. We may hear that Word with joy and find strength in him to obey.

When we see him as Lord, we realize that whatever the Word says to us, we are to commit ourselves to it.

When we see him as present with us, we realize he has not left us to struggle alone. He himself takes up every burden and bears it for us. When we see him as *this kind of God*, we are moved to love him, and through love we are moved to obey.

And so we come full circle.

In obedience, we feel his touch. We know his working in our lives and come to love him even more.

This is our ministry to each other in the small group. To help each other see Jesus and all he is for us. And to help each other love and trust him even more.

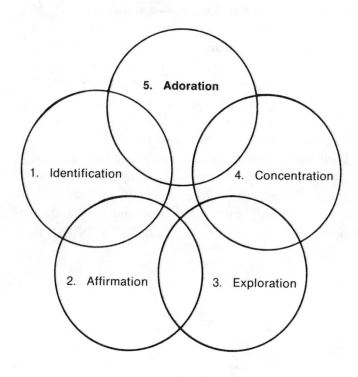

Essential Elements

1. Identification
2. Affirmation
3. Exploration
4. Concentration
5. Adoration

6

adoration

We know little of worship these days. So often our church services, after a few hymns, concentrate on proclamation of the Word and exhortation but then fall short of leading us on to worship God.

I think probably I first experienced worship in seminary. Not in the classes or in our daily chapels, but in a motel near campus where I worked at night. There I found time to study the Bible. I started working through my New Testament, using the language tools I was gaining in my daytime studies, and I began to discover in fresh and new ways what God was communicating to me. It was really unexpected. But again and again I found that after I had dug into the Bible for an hour or two, without any planning or effort, I found myself praying and simply thanking God for who he is.

I've had similar experiences in our church. In one congregation we had a time of sharing after the sermon. The family shared their week—prayer requests, burdens, answers to prayer, joys. There, too, as in the Bible study, I often found myself worshiping unexpectedly.

Later I learned that my experience harmonized with basic Bible teachings about worship. Worship is both *affirming God,* and *responding to his self-revelation.*

Affirming God

There's reason to believe that worship is our primary and perhaps most significant response to the Lord. Paul presents as evidence of the terrible corruption sin brings the fact that when men knew what could be known about God in creation, "they neither glorified him as God nor gave thanks to him" (Rom. 1:21). Whenever we sense God, we are to express our praise, our thanks, and tell him how good and wonderful he is.

The Book of Psalms teaches us how to praise. Psalm 145, for instance, highlights characteristics of the Lord that thrill the psalmist and captures his sense of awe, wonder, and joy.

PSALM 145

A psalm of praise. Of David.

[1] I will exalt you, my God the King;
I will praise your name for ever and ever.
[2] Every day I will praise you
and extol your name for ever and ever.
[3] Great is the Lord and most worthy of praise;
his greatness no one can fathom.
[4] One generation will commend your works to another;
They will tell of your mighty acts.
[5] They will speak of the glorious splendor of
your majesty, and I will meditate on your
wonderful works.
[6] They will tell of the power of your awesome works,
and I will proclaim your great deeds.
[7] They will celebrate your abundant goodness
and joyfully sing of your righteousness.
[8] The Lord is gracious and compassionate,
slow to anger and rich in love.
[9] The Lord is good to all;
he has compassion on all he has made.

¹⁰All you have made will praise you, O LORD;
your saints will extol you.
¹¹They will tell of the glory of your kingdom
and speak of your might,
¹²So that all men may know of your mighty acts
and the glorious splendor of your kingdom.
¹³Your kingdom is an everlasting kingdom,
and your dominion endures through all
generations.
The LORD is faithful to all his promises
and loving toward all he has made.
¹⁴The LORD upholds all those who fall
and lifts up all who are bowed down.
¹⁵The eyes of all look to you,
and you give them their food at the proper time.
¹⁶You open your hand
and satisfy the desires of every living thing.
¹⁷The LORD is righteous in all his ways
and loving toward all he has made.
¹⁸The LORD is near to all who call on him,
to all who call on him in truth.
¹⁹He fulfills the desires of those who fear him;
he hears their cry and saves them.
²⁰The LORD watches over all who love him,
but all the wicked he will destroy.
²¹My mouth will speak in praise of the LORD.
Let every creature praise his holy name
for ever and ever.

As we come to know him, such spontaneous expressions are called out from us. Individually and together we are to praise God for who he, by nature, is.

Such worship is an essential part of the life of a group that meets for ministry because it is an essential part of every person's personal relationship with the Lord. A ministry group meets to deepen relationships, not simply horizontal relationships between members of the body of Christ, but also the vertical relationships between each participant and the Lord. However, these two relationships are interwoven. As we come to appreciate each other and what God is doing in our lives, we sense God's presence. And as we share together in praise, we are drawn closer to each other.

The fact is that the foundation of our relationships with other Christians is and must be laid on Jesus. We can be one and experience unity only because we *are* one in Christ. Jesus himself, then, must be the focus and the center of our shared life. While worship is essentially for God's benefit, worshiping the Lord with others does benefit us as well. We are drawn closer to each other as we draw closer, together, to the Lord.

Response to God

I've noted that worship is affirming God. It is expressing to him our praise, our appreciation, our wonder, our approval for who he is.

It is just as important to realize that worship is a *response* to God's self-revelation. Worship isn't something we can program—something we "turn on" with stately music. Worship is a response to God himself and comes whenever the believer meets him afresh—when God reveals himself to us. So, worship may come at any time during our meeting for ministry when God's presence is sensed, but it can seldom be "programmed."

There are two primary channels of God's self-revelation in our small-group meetings: the Word and one another!

The Word. This is, of course, the primary channel through which God has chosen to reveal himself to us. Thus, worship in our group normally will follow sharing in the Word. It will come more spontaneously and more meaningfully after the group has focused on the Lord and what he has to say to them. While most church services seem to expect people to worship *before* meeting God in the preached Word, we shouldn't make this mistake in our meeting for ministry.

As I said, we *expect* to meet God afresh in the Word. But there is another aspect of God's self-revelation that is important when we meet for ministry.

Meeting God in one another. We remember that the purpose of meeting for ministry is to help one another grow toward Christlikeness. This is something the apostle Paul wrote of in 2 Corinthians 3, "You yourselves are our letter, written on our hearts, known and read by everybody. You show that you are a letter from Christ, the result of our ministry, written not with ink but with the Spirit of the living God, not on tablets of stone but on tablets of human hearts" (2 Cor. 3:2–3). In others words, God is at work, writing his Word in our living personalities!

Paul continues to draw a fascinating contrast. Looking back to the time of Moses, he notes that after Moses had spent time with the Lord, his face shone with a special radiance. But that radiance faded when Moses left the Lord's presence. To keep the Israelites from seeing that the radiance was fading away, Moses "would put a veil over his face." Paul, however, says that we have a unique hope, and because of it we are "not like Moses!" We Christians take the veils off, freely sharing who and what we are. As Paul explains,

> Now the Lord is the Spirit, and where the Spirit of the Lord is, there is freedom. And we, who with unveiled faces all reflect the Lord's glory, are being transformed into his likeness with ever-increasing glory, which comes from the Lord who is the Spirit.
>
> (2 Cor. 3:17–18)

Paul's point is important. We Christians are *always* in the presence of the Lord, for the Holy Spirit of God lives within us. And the Spirit of God is at work in us to transform us "with ever-increasing glory" into Jesus' own likeness. As a result, when we take the veils off and live honestly with each other, we see in each other's faces a reflection of the Lord!

It's vital we don't misunderstand. Jesus' presence is seen not in our perfection, but in our progress. It is not who we are, but who we are becoming that reveals the reality of Jesus.

When we meet for ministry and share out of our humanity, we see Jesus at work in each of our lives. And in this revelation of Jesus in us, as well as the revelation of Jesus in Scripture, God does meet us.

How rich an experience when we gather weekly to hear how each of us has experienced Jesus' touch during the week. And how exciting to see him *alive* through his working in the life of a brother or sister whom we are coming to love.

While hymns and stately buildings, or nature itself, may turn our hearts to the Lord and stimulate worship, his primary means of self-revelation remain the Word of God and the lives of believers. *And these two primary sources are exactly what meeting for ministry provides!*

When we meet for ministry, then, and when we see the Lord in the Word or each other, we need to be sensitive enough to stop, to speak directly to the Lord, and to give him our praise and worship.

Meeting for ministry, then, can be one of the most enriching experiences for Christians. In the context of shared lives and the dynamic of those spiritual processes, which make small groups vital and alive, we *can* grow together toward the likeness of Christ.

And we can help each other grow in this way; it's God's own goal for you and me.

PART 2:

ACTION IDEAS

ACTION IDEAS

Launching Small Groups

It's important to begin ministry groups well and to keep in touch with them as the group climate develops. Don't try to get "everyone" involved in a small group; instead, focus on locating those who sense a personal need and seem eager to participate. Here are some action ideas to help church leaders launch small groups in a local congregational setting.

1. *Sign-up card*

Put a sign-up card in your church bulletin to be deposited in the offering plate by those interested. Contact those who respond and schedule a time to get together and talk about forming a group. The card might say something like this:

Fellowship

Have you felt lonely or wanted closer relationships with other Christians? Are you eager to deepen your relationship with Jesus? One way to meet both these needs is to *meet for ministry* with a small group of others who feel the same way. If you're interested, drop this card in the offering plate or mail it to the church this week. We'll be in contact.

Name _____

Age _____

Address _____

Phone _____

2. *New ideas for groups*

Where you have no tradition of small groups, try new *short-term structures* in regular activities. For instance, try a three-week "special" study program for your weeknight service. Prepare a study sheet (like those illustrated in this section) and break into small groups for sharing and study. Or try a special six-week Sunday school elective using participative methods. The more experience Christians have in small groups, the more open some of them will be to participating in a small group.

3. *Transformation*

We can help Christians become sensitive to their needs for the kind of relationships small groups encourage. To do this, we need to show a concern in church ministries for what God is doing in persons. That is, we need to keep our focus on God's goal— transformation.

Communication is the key. In one church, the pastor featured a "God at work" spot each Sunday, in which he had a *brief* dialogue at the pulpit with a person whose life God had touched in some way during the week. In another church, a newsletter featured a "God at work" column that reported significant experiences in members' lives. This kind of communication helped the congregation realize that God truly was at work among them and created an eagerness for a deeper personal experience with Christ that led to small groups.

4. *Planning a retreat*

Usually it's most effective to launch small groups with a retreat. A good retreat will have two powerful benefits. First, it will quickly establish the closer personal relationships that need to be developed for a ministry group to succeed. And second, it will in

SCHEDULE

FRIDAY		SATURDAY	
Arrival	6:30	Breakfast	7:30
Settled in	7:00	Sharing (whole group)	8:00
Building acquaintances (8s)	7:05	Team creativity	9:00
Snack break	9:05	Sharing by teams	11:00
Studying together	9:25	Lunch	11:45
Lights out	11:00	Studying together	1:00
		Sharing goals/worship	3:00
		Departure	4:15

effect train the small group how to function effectively in a ministry setting.

On the previous page is a retreat plan for launching a small-group ministry that can be adapted to any local church.

The retreat

The retreat itself should involve all members of newly formed groups and should plan to involve eight to ten members who will be the nucleus of a new group sharing experiences together. As many groups as you wish may be formed and launched at a single retreat, and if possible, they should only be launched during a retreat setting.

Building acquaintances

The following pattern helps group members learn about each other and also helps individuals begin to reveal things about themselves in a nonthreatening context. This initiation to self-revelation is very important.

- Place participants in the groups where they will be after the retreat. Divide into pairs within each group. Each person is to tell his partner "all he needs to know" to understand him as a person in three minutes. Then these roles are reversed.
- Next, the small groups come together, and each person has one and a half minutes to help the group understand his partner as a person. Everyone is free to interject questions and comments, and the group's time should be permitted to extend over the suggested limit.
- Each group member is then asked to check his perception of other members by saying what he thinks they were like at age seven. One of the

group is selected as the first subject. Each then shares his impression of the subject-person as a seven year old. The subject is invited to tell what the group saw correctly and incorrectly. In the process, he begins to share more about himself. Each person takes turns being a subject.

- At this point each member is asked to recall himself at age seventeen and imagine this situation: *At seventeen I developed serious questions about my faith. How would I handle my doubts? Share them? With whom? Hide them? Suppress them? Why?* Here, too, conversation within the group is encouraged, as each person begins to reveal how he tends to handle socially unacceptable thoughts and feelings.
- The retreat leader concludes this segment by reading 2 Corinthians 1:3–11 and showing the importance of being ourselves and expressing ourselves if we are to minister to one another.

Groups meet together and do the following Bible study, adapted from a Serendipity study developed by Lyman Coleman. Each step is to be taken in sequence, with no looking ahead by members of the group. A properly folded sheet permits this easily and naturally, at a pace set by the group members themselves. *The sketches and numbered exercises on the next page explain this Bible study.*

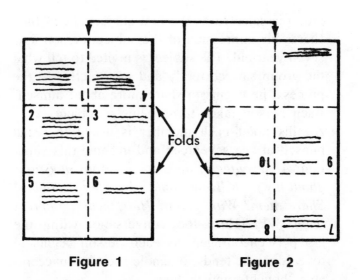

Figure 1

Figure 2

a. Fold 5 and 6 up behind 2 and 3. b. Fold 1 and 4 down and over 5 and 6. c. Fold 2 over 3.

This is the reverse side of the Bible study sheet before it is folded.

Figure 3

The Bible study sheet, when folded properly, looks like this and is ready to use.

1. Read the Bible passage in exercise 2. Think about the man described. What kind of person is he?

Picture yourself as a psychiatrist, developing a case history. From what you see in the Bible text (the man's past, present associations, etc.), what kind of person would you say he was when Jesus first spoke to him?

Turn to exercise 2 and spend ten to fifteen minutes developing your "case history."

2. ²Now there is in Jerusalem near the Sheep Gate a pool, which in Aramaic is called Bethesda and which is surrounded by five covered colonnades. ³Here a great number of disabled people used to lie—the blind, the lame, the paralyzed. ⁵One who was there had been an invalid for thirty-eight years. ⁶When Jesus saw him lying there and learned that he had been in this condition for a long time, he asked him, "Do you want to get well?"

⁷"Sir," the invalid replied, "I have no one to help me into the pool when the water is stirred. While I am trying to get in, someone else goes down ahead of me."

[8] Then Jesus said to him, "Get up! Take up your mat and walk." [9] At once the man was cured; he picked up his mat and walked.

(John 5:2–9)

3. Case history notes.

When completed, turn together to exercise 4.

4. Now, let each member of the group share his insights.

Particularly, talk together about why Jesus might have asked, "Do you *want* to be healed?"

You do not have to agree, so don't try to win others to your understanding of the man. Simply explore the possibilities, share your ideas, and listen to each other.

Continue discussion for twenty minutes. When finished, open the sheet to exercise 5.

5. Jesus is as real today as he was by Bethesda. He is just as able to heal and to transform. And we are in as great a need as the sick man. Jesus asks us the same kind of probing, challenging question:
    "Do you want to be healed?"
If Jesus were to ask you this question now, what in your life would he most likely be speaking of?

Allow three to five minutes to jot down likely possibilities.

6. My own "infirmities"?

When all are finished, begin together exercise 7, which is on the reverse side of the study sheet.

7. Now have each person share the thing or things you pinpointed as personal needs or infirmities.

    Take as long as you need to understand fully what each person is sharing.

    Then turn down the flap to do exercises 9 and 10 together.

8. Notes on what each shares.

9. Giving gifts.

When Jesus saw the need of the man by the pool, he gave him a gift that met his need.

What gift would you like to give each member of your group in Jesus' name?

Think for a moment of what each person has shared. Jot down a gift by each name that reveals what you believe Jesus wants to do for that person. In turn around the circle, let everyone give the gifts to each person.

10. The gifts I give . . . and receive.

When the gifts have been given, join hands and pray for each other as your time of community draws to a close.

99

All on the retreat share breakfast. For devotions after the meal, each person shares a verse of Scripture and explains why that verse is important. Each person is limited to 30 seconds for his sharing.

Team creativity

Divide again into the functioning small groups (8s or 10s). If you are in a camp retreat setting, have group members use materials they can find outdoors. If in a motel or other indoor setting, bring a variety of materials—paper, picture magazines, etc. Each group is to use the materials to create *together* a model or a poster of "God's work in our lives."

Encourage group members to spend at least thirty minutes talking together about how God works in persons, what he does, where he begins, what his goals are, and how his work can be recognized. Then working together, find ways to build a model or represent on a poster what the group has talked of, while letting additional thoughts find creative expression as the project is being developed.

Stress that this is to be a team project: Each person should feel that he makes a significant contribution to the creation of the whole.

Team sharing

When projects are completed, each small group should share with the whole group by showing and explaining its model or poster. Either a designated individual or each member of the team may be asked to explain a particular feature of the completed creation.

God's creation

Spend the afternoon studying in the small groups, using the same procedure as detailed in the ten-step study shown on the preceding pages. This particular study focuses on God's work of creation and the ways in which he shows by what he has created (1) how important people are to him and (2) how he communicates specialness to us.

The following sketches and numbered diagrams explain the Bible study about God's creation.

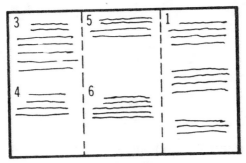

Figure 4

The Bible study sheet is folded accordian-style so that exercise 1 is visible.

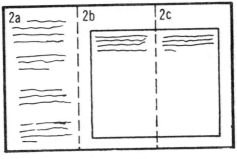

Figure 5

The reverse side of the study sheet shows exercise 2 and the chart panels accompanying it.

1

The Bible says only of man, "God created man in his own image, in the image of God created he him; male and female created he them" (Gen. 1:27, KJV).

People were, and are, very special to God.

Jot down here one way that you feel you are special.

_____

_____

_____

_____

Record one additional thing that you like about yourself, one other thing that makes you feel like a special and worthwhile person.

_____

_____

_____

_____

THEN

Share with one another (allow 10–15 minutes) what you recorded before you turn to exercise 2.

2a

Read the following verses from Genesis 2, which show how God communicated to man that people are special to him, and complete the chart panels. (Study individually for 10–15 minutes.)

7 And the Lord God formed man of the dust of the ground, and breathed into his nostrils the breath of life; and man became a living soul.

8 And the Lord God planted a garden eastward in Eden; and there he put the man whom he had formed. 9 And out of the ground made the Lord God to grow every tree that is pleasant to the sight, and good for food.

15 And the Lord God took the man, and put him into the garden of Eden to dress it and to keep it. 16 And the Lord God commanded the man, saying, Of every tree of the garden thou mayest freely eat: 17 But of the tree of the knowledge of good and evil, thou shalt not eat of it: for in the day that thou eatest thereof thou shalt surely die.

18 And the Lord God said, It is not good that the man should be alone; I will make him an help meet for him.

19 And out of the ground the Lord God formed every beast of the field, and every fowl of the air; and brought them unto Adam to see what he would call them: and whatsoever Adam called every living creature, that was the name thereof.

20 But for Adam there was not found an help meet for him. 21 And the Lord God caused a deep sleep to fall upon Adam, and he slept: and he took one of his ribs, and closed up the flesh instead thereof; 22 And from the rib, which the Lord God had taken from man, made he a woman, and brought her unto the man. 23 And Adam said, This is now bone of my bones, and flesh of my flesh.

2b

What need of man does God recognize
and act to meet?

2c

How does God's action affirm that people are important to him?

3

Select one of God's actions discovered in the study in exercise 2 that seems to you to communicate best a sense of God's love to you. Share with the group what this action is and why you chose it. (Allow 15–20 minutes for all to share.)

4

From what your group members have all shared about how love is communicated to them, see if you can decide together some effective ways to help each other realize that each person is really special to God and worth loving by the group as well. (Allow 20–30 minutes.)

How we can communicate love

1.
2.
3.
4.
5.
6.
7.
8.
9.
10.

5

Affirm one another—communicate to each person that we appreciate him and see him as special to us.

From your time together, jot down the first name of each person in your group and write one way in which he seems special to you. When all have finished, begin with one member of the group and, speaking directly to him, let each person say, " _____, I appreciate you because . . ."

Continue in this way with each group member sharing (no time limit).

6

Close with prayer, thanking God for his love and for one another.

Call everyone on the retreat together for closing worship. All join hands to form a linked circle to share in an open time of prayer. Tell the Lord why you came on this retreat and wanted to become a member of a small group and thank him for progress toward the goal you have felt on the weekend. Intersperse worship and praise choruses and songs with the prayer, and conclude by singing "They'll Know We Are Christians by Our Love."

5. *Questionnaire*

As a group continues to meet, it's important to keep in touch with how the group members see and feel about its gatherings. Here's a questionnaire that each member might fill out after the fourth of fifth meeting of a new group.

Mark each statement with an S (I am generally satisfied with our progress and relationship), U (I am unsatisfied with our progress or relationship), or D (I have no feelings on this subject either way).

_____ (1)   I am getting to know and appreciate others in our group.

_____ (2)   I feel free to express myself in the group.

_____ (3)   I feel others are expressing their real feelings and letting me come to know them in a meaningful way.

_____ (4)   There is no individual or individuals with whom I am uncertain or by whom I sometimes feel disliked.

_____ (5)   I feel that most members of the group can and do understand me and the things I have to share.

_____ (6)   I have felt really welcome in the group.

_____ (7)   I have found it easy to express appreciation and approval of others in the group.

_____ (8)   I feel the others in the group really like and accept me.

_____ (9)   I have actually told someone (in or after a group meeting) that I care about and am praying for him.

_____ (10)   I have been told by members of the group that they care about and are praying for me.

_____ (11)   I am learning things about God that I did not understand before.

_____ (12)   I feel that our Bible studies are more than just learning information because they involve discovery of what the Word means to me.

_____ (13)   I feel all members of the group are contributing to our understanding of what the Bible says and means to us.

_____ (14)   I think the Bible is playing the role it ought to in our group.

_____ (15)   I am satisfied with the methods and approach to Bible study we are using now.

_____ (16)   I sense an optimism in the group and an expectation that Christ will really work in us.

_____ (17)   We are sharing meaningful things that the Lord is doing in our lives.

_____ (18)   I am coming to realize how powerful and close Jesus is to me.

_____ (19)   I think other members of the group are also seeing Christ as more powerful and real than they did before.

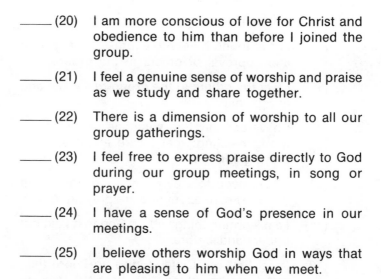

_____ (20) I am more conscious of love for Christ and obedience to him than before I joined the group.

_____ (21) I feel a genuine sense of worship and praise as we study and share together.

_____ (22) There is a dimension of worship to all our group gatherings.

_____ (23) I feel free to express praise directly to God during our group meetings, in song or prayer.

_____ (24) I have a sense of God's presence in our meetings.

_____ (25) I believe others worship God in ways that are pleasing to him when we meet.

The questionnaire may be used in a variety of ways. Each unit of five questions is, obviously, correlated with one of the five vital elements of group life. You may (a) discuss each cluster of five items as a unit and note any areas in which several group members feel a weakness; (b) discuss the questionnaire item by item, letting each express his evaluation and explain reasons for feelings not shared by others in the group; (c) collect the questionnaires and collate the answers, then plan to use one or more Action Ideas to strengthen the area in which the group members sense weakness; (d) locate interpersonal tensions by having each person add on the left the name or names of group members who seem to be the reason for an unsatisfactory experience. This, too, may be collated, and all the information given to every group member for discussion at the next meeting. Or if an individual finds one name recurring on the questionnaire (a very likely occurrence), he may be encouraged to get together with that person during the week to express his feelings and attempt to resolve the problem (cf. Matt. 5:23, 24).

6. *Group feedback*

After a number of weeks together, spend five sessions restudying the central chapters of this book (2–6). Have each member prepare by reading an agreed-on chapter and having ready some specific examples of ways that the group has included that element (Identification, Affirmation, Exploration, Concentration, or Adoration), or ways that a weakness in the area exists.

For group feedback to be effective, it is important that each person share honestly what he feels about the situation, and that each seek lovingly to help one another grow toward God's goal for his body of Christ.

7. *Paired feedback*

Sometimes, it is easier for people to give feedback if they feel others share their perceptions. For paired feedback, give out the questionnaire (No. 5) but ask members of the group to meet in pairs before the next session to discuss their responses. When both members of a pair see something in the same light (either a strong positive or a strong negative), they covenant to share their feelings with the whole group at the next meeting.

8. *Individual feedback*

Give each group member a 3x5 or 4x6 card, one side of which is marked with a large plus (+), the other side of which is marked with a large minus (−). Each group member is to fill out each side of the card, completing the following statements.

+ *The greatest benefit of the group to me has been . . .*

and
- *My biggest disappointment about the group has been . . .*

If an individual does not feel strongly about either a plus or minus, he need not fill out that side of the card.

When all are completed, begin at random and have the first person read a plus and explain why he has written what he has. The next person, moving to his right, then reads a minus and again explains why he has written what he has. Individuals may be questioned and their perceptions discussed by the group.

Another way: all the pluses, or all the minuses, may be read aloud, and then the feelings of the whole group discussed as they have been revealed in the report. Be sure to conclude such a session with a discussion of steps to strengthen the group and realize God's purpose in you.

IDENTIFICATION

Here are some things you may do in a small group to get to know each other better. Some encourage sharing on the level of our common humanity; others stress our experience with Christ; still others emphasize sharing on both levels. Use these when you begin a group or when you feel your sense of identity with each other is slipping.

9. *What has my life been like?*
Graph your spiritual experience.

Many Christians find their lives marked by ups and downs. Give each member of the group paper and crayons to graph the peaks and valleys of his life.

Variations. Make the graph represent the whole life, before and after conversion. Or make the graph represent only experience as a Christian. The pattern may be then shared with and explained to the group by each member.

For greater depth. Have members specifically label each peak and valley (or the most significant ones). Discuss these in greater depth as all seek to understand one another better.

10. *Where am I now?*

Explain the two circles used in chapter 2 to illustrate our dual identity. Ask each person to draw two circles representing himself, indicating where he feels he is right now in terms of experiencing Christ's adequacy.

For instance, one might feel he is far from knowing the meaning of Christ in his life and thus draw the circles as barely touching. Another might feel more encouraged and draw considerable overlap.

After each person has drawn his own diagram, he explains what he has drawn and why he feels this portrays him. The group is free to interact with the one who is sharing and may share in return.

11. *Are others really like me?*

Give paper and pen to each group member and ask him to take five to eight minutes to describe an experience or situation that made an impact on who he is as a person, but which he has felt was so unusual that few could understand or identify with it. After the descriptions have been written, have each person list on the back of the paper the feelings he associates with the experience.

Then have individuals read their descriptions. After each is read, other members of the group should say what feelings they believe are associated with that experience. The one who reads then reports the feelings he has listed on the back of his paper and explains them. For greater depth, after each person's sharing, have other group members tell of times when they felt like the reader.

12. *How do I experience Christ?*

Have each member of the group jot down quickly five times when Jesus seemed very real and close to him. Take turns around the group; share the five. As each person shares his list, the group members should look for a pattern. For instance, one person might list instances of sorrow or tragedy. Group members might note this and suggest, "You seem to see Jesus as someone very warm and loving and look to him for comfort." Or "You really must trust him a lot. When things like that happen to me, I get mad. But you still sense his love."

Another group member might list instances of recovery after failures or sins. Group members would note for him, "You seem to see Jesus as a real overcomer, someone who turns your life around."

It's exciting to realize that Jesus can and does meet all our needs. This kind of sharing should help the group see the Lord's adequacy in a fresh way and develop identity with others as those who share Christ's life, too.

13. *Quickie reentry activities*

Sometimes, a short time of sharing at the beginning of a group session will reestablish or remind of identity already established. Here are several incomplete sentences group members may be invited to complete with the first thought that comes to mind. Start off a group session with these, using one to three per session.

(a) One word that describes my week is . . .

(b) Right now I feel . . .

(c) To me Jesus is like . . .

(d) I'm happy about . . .

(e) I'm sad about . . .

(f) One thing I really like about myself today is . . .

(g) One thing I don't like about myself today is . . .

(h) I'm thankful that . . .

(i) Life gets _____ all the time.

(j) What I want most from life right now is . . .

(k) One thing I enjoyed doing this week was . . .

(l) One thing I did today because I had to was . . .

(m) Today what I'd like to change about myself is . . .

(n) The biggest evidence that Jesus is in me now is . . .

(o) I feel like (select an animal and tell why) . . .

14. *Self-portrait*

Give each participant a large sheet of oaktag paper (or light posterboard) and crayon. Each is to draw a design (using colors and shapes as he wishes) to represent himself, as seen right now.

When completed, each is to show his self-portrait to the group and explain the picture in detail. Questions may be asked by the group.

15. *Ideal self-portrait*

Give out crayons and oaktag. But this time ask each person to portray himself as he *wants to be,* that is, portray the ideal self.

Again, when completed each person should share and explain the picture.

16. *Strength recognition exercise*

Tape to the wall large sheets of newsprint, one for each member of a small group. Give each person a felt-tipped pen. On his sheet a person is to record, beginning with childhood, every "success" he can remember. Allow thirty minutes for this part of the activity.

When everyone is finished, one member sits near the center of the group, and all the others examine what he has recorded on his sheet. The group is to examine the recorded successes and discuss, while the subject remains silent, these questions: (1) What constitutes success _____ ? [For some, it may be personal or artistic achievement, sports, making money, or friendship development.] (2) What strengths does the chart reveal _____ ? (3) What possible warnings or dangers are indicated?

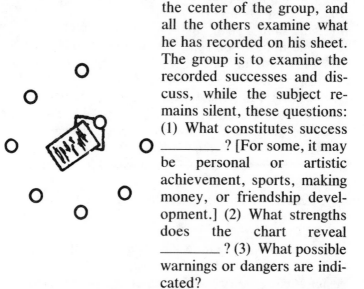

After discussion is completed, the person may respond as he wishes. Then, another member of the group shows his list, and so on.

When this activity is completed, the group should

be reminded, "God has made each of us special, with our own unique gifts and talents. But we can't depend on these abilities alone. Even our strengths may become weaknesses. Yet, Christ's power is available to flow through us and vitalize every strength and talent for his glory and for the benefit of other people."

The group may pause for prayer or start the next Bible study.

17. *Bible character*

Ask each person to select a Bible character whom they feel is like them. In turn around the circle, ask each to identify that Bible person, and share why he is like that person.

18. *Family stories*

Ask each person to tell a story from childhood that reveals something important about his family. After the story is told, from the story let each person in turn make one comment about the storyteller's feelings about childhood, relationship with parents, the family's influence, etc. Afterward, the storyteller should respond, telling which comments were accurate reflections and which comments were not.

In the early stages of group life, it's often helpful to take opening time to "get to know" one member. An activity like this might be used with one group member each week until all have had a chance to tell a story.

19. *Psalms reflection*

At the beginning of a group time, ask each person to thumb through the psalms and find one verse that reflects how he feels that evening. These can be read without comment and will make group members more sensitive to each other's needs as the evening progresses.

20. *New people*

When a new person comes to the group for the first time, introduce the regulars this way. Have the leader begin and select one person, whom he introduces to the newcomer. The introduction is to stress why this person is important to the introducer or what special contribution he makes to the group life. After being introduced, the person selects someone else to introduce. Continue until each member of the group has been introduced in this way.

This simple activity will communicate the mutual love that characterizes your relationships as well as help that newcomer identify individuals.

The group member who brought the newcomer should explain the guest's importance as a way of introduction.

21. *Childhood stories*

Often, talking about childhood is less threatening to an individual than speaking about now. You can do a number of "childhood" activities that will help your group members feel comfortable talking with each other and gradually build not only understanding of one another but also increasing freedom for openness.

Here are a few starters to ask each person in the group to share. Feel free to be creative in thinking up some to fit your group's needs.

- As a third grader, I was . . .
- The place I liked best in my house was . . .
- What was most likely to make me mad was . . .
- What I liked best to do with my mom was . . .
- I felt most alone as a child when . . .

22. *Tags*

Have colored tags available as group members enter. Each is to select a tag that represents how the week went. As you begin, ask the "blues" to share what happened, then the "reds," etc.

23. *Partners*

Pair off and ask each person to find out three things not yet known about the partner. Then come together and have each person share what was learned about the partner.

24. *Describing your week*

Have each person select a four-letter word that describes the week. Then make an acrostic: Build descriptive sentences on its letters to sum up the reason for the feelings. For instance, a person who wrote GOOD to describe the week might write these reasons:

> God really helped me this week,
> Others were helpful, too.
> Over and over compliments came to me,
> Delighting my heart and making me thankful.

Taking turns, each person reads the acrostic.

25. *Ups and downs*

Pick a Bible person who experienced ups and downs, such as David. Work as a group to brainstorm a timeline of his experiences—shepherd boy, facing Goliath, married to king's daughter, running from Saul, made king, victorious in battle, sinning with Bathsheba, forgiven by God, heartbroken at Absalom's rebellion, restored to the throne, etc.

Then ask each person to say where his experience just now seems to be like something that happened to David.

26. *Games*

Take an evening out and play a game that helps members come to know each other better. One of the best is the *Ungame,* which can be purchased at most toy stores. There is also a set of "Christian" cards available for it.

27. *Body language*

Be sensitive to body language. After your group members have chatted at the opening of a session, stop and ask, "Has anyone noticed anything that suggests how another person might be feeling this evening?"

Encourage people to say what they may have noticed. For instance, "Jim seems to be smiling a lot tonight. I guess he's had a pretty good day." Or, "Helen, I've noticed that you're sitting back in your chair and not talking much. You seem to keep looking away from us, too. Is something wrong?"

After you've done these "body language checks" several times in a few months, your group members will become more and more sensitive to clues for other's feelings.

AFFIRMATION

It is important as you meet for ministry to affirm each other. There are a number of things you can do not only to help group members come to know each other better, but also to communicate love and appreciation to each other. Here are some Action Ideas that will help your group members grow in their ability to affirm one another in a positive way.

28. *What am I like?*

Pin a sheet of paper to the back of each group member. Have each write on the others' backs one positive word that best seems to describe the individual.

When this is completed, each person takes his sheet of paper and, looking at what the others have written, writes a brief statement of "What I am like." Each then reads aloud what he has written and gives all the group members opportunity both to add to what has been written and to affirm points that seem particularly significant to them.

29. *How am I important?*

Ask each member of the group to write the names of all the other members. Beside each name should be listed one or more positive ways he contributes to the meaningfulness of your time together. When this has been written, one person is seated in a chair placed slightly in toward the center of the encircling group. Then each person takes a turn speaking directly to the person in the center, saying, "I'm glad you're in our group ..." and telling the contribution he listed.

It is important that this affirmation be directed to the individual rather than the group. Don't speak *about* the person in the center; speak *to* him.

In conclusion, it may seem appropriate to join hands and pray together or sing a meaningful hymn.

30. *Exploring affirmation*

Pair the group members and assign one or more of the following verses to each pair:

Romans 12:10	Ephesians 4:2
Romans 15:7 (14:1)	Ephesians 4:32
Romans 15:14	Hebrews 10:24
1 Corinthians 12:25	1 Peter 1:22
Galatians 6:2	1 Peter 5:5

The two are to study the verse and context together and discuss how the situation in Scripture demonstrated affirmation of one another. Then each pair is to agree on at least two other persons in the group who perform this ministry to group members. After twenty minutes, bring everyone back together. Have each pair read the verse and speak to the individual they chose, saying, "Jon, we've seen you affirm in this way. When you told Mary last week . . . And when you said . . ."

When all have shared, spend time in prayer simply thanking God for the gifts he has given you in each other.

31. *I can grow*

This activity expresses trust in other members of the group, and at the same time points up weaknesses that need to be dealt with. It involves affirming by reproof!

Give each group member a number of 3x5 cards. On each, the individual is to write the name of a member of the group, then on the back complete the following sentence: "I want to see you grow, and trust you to grow, in . . ." Anything that a person sees as an area of need may be mentioned.

". . . in your freedom to accept yourself."

". . . in your ability to control your temper."

". . . in being free of the feeling that someone is attacking you all the time."

". . . in your willingness to accept others, and not act as though you have to make them see things your way."

More than one 3x5 card may be completed for a group member, but each should fill out at least one card for every person. When the cards are finished, each person should be given those about him. Each then may look through the cards and set aside (1) any that puzzle or disturb him and (2) groups of three or more cards that suggest the same area for growth.

In turn, each person reads aloud the cards that puzzle him or show that several in the group see him in a similar light. The person reading should then tell how he feels about what is on the card, and he is free to ask the group, or individuals in the group, *why* they wrote down what they did.

As each individual finishes, the group should take time immediately to pray for him and for the needs explored, both thanking God for the person as he is and thanking God that he is at work in that individual's life, freeing him to grow and to become in Christ.

32. *I am growing*

Have group members spontaneously tell each other the growth they have seen in the time the group has been together and how seeing God at work in specific individuals has ministered to them personally.

33. *Portraits*

Give out oaktag or 8 1/2 x 11″ sheets of paper and crayons. Select one person to focus on, and have everyone draw a design (using colors and shapes) to represent that person, as he has been, is now, and is becoming.

When completed, each should show the portrait and explain it thoroughly.

34. *Identification*

Speak to another person, saying, "You remind me of . . ." and quote either a Bible verse or name a Bible character. Then explain how that person reminds you of the verse or Bible person.

You can focus on one person or go through the group, letting a person named pick another and repeat, "You remind me of . . ."

35. *One worders*

Ask each group member to jot down *one word* that in a positive way expresses how he perceives one or more others. Sometime during the group session or just after it, each person is to share his one word with the other(s) he selected.

36. *Flower building*

Select one group member to receive special affirmation each week. Cut petals from colored construction paper. Have a variety of colors available. Draw the leaves and stalk of a flower on a sturdy sheet of paper.

In the group have each person select a colored petal that represents an area of growth in the individual to be affirmed. Have that person hold the sheet of paper, and group members take turns selecting a colored petal to add to the "flower" being built on the stalk. As each petal is added, the person should tell the strength or positive quality it represents, and how this has been seen in the affirmed person's life.

The person affirmed can take the completed flower home, as a reminder of how the group appreciates him.

37. *Experiencing welcome*

Different persons experience love and welcome in different ways. Go around the circle and ask how each one most likes to be greeted—with a smile, a hug, a wave, by stopping to talk, etc.

Encourage other group members to give the kind of greeting that each person experiences as true welcome.

38. *Self-affirmation*

One of the most significant steps a person can take is to express to others positive things about himself.

Growth in self-acceptance and in ability to appreciate oneself can be important not only for growth as a person but also for spiritual growth, for we human beings have been made in the image of God and are to love ourselves as well as God and others.

So, have each person tell one thing he really likes about himself. Or relate "one good thing" he did this week.

39. *Phone notes*

Encourage each group member to telephone one person the next week with a word of appreciation for something about him that has been helpful in the caller's Christian experience.

40. *Appreciation cards*

Have appreciation postcards available each week. Encourage group members to take some and jot notes of thanks to other members for any qualities or acts that prove to be helpful during the coming week.

41. *Group affirmation*

It's important not only to express appreciation for individuals in a group that meets for ministry, but also for the group itself. Focus on what participation means to each individual, now and then, using any of these or other starter phrases.

- Belonging to this group . . .
- What I like best about our group is . . .
- I feel accepted here because . . .
- Meeting together for ministry is like . . .

42. *Affirming Bible study: Genesis 1*

Many passages in Scripture communicate how important we are as individuals to God. One is detailed earlier in action idea 4, and can be used as a group study in a regular meeting, as well as in a retreat setting.

43. *Affirming Bible study: Ephesians 1–2*

Explore your identity as Christians by looking through Ephesians 1–2. Look first for active verbs that tell what God has done for us. (See Eph. 1:5, 8, 13; 2:5, 6, 8, 13, 19, 22.) Then read again to find out what we have now in him. (See Eph. 1:6, 7, 9, 13, 18, 19, 23; 2:4, 5, 13, 14, 16, 18, 19, 20, 22.)

After listing discoveries, ask each person to write down a brief paragraph stating, "Who am I."

Read the paragraphs to each other and discuss what each person found in these chapters about who we are as Jesus' people, what seems most important to each personally, and why.

44. *Affirming Bible study: 1 Peter 1:22*

The verse states: "Now that you have purified yourself by obeying the truth so that you have sincere love for your brothers, love one another deeply, from the heart."

Ask each to meditate on the verse. Then discuss these questions: How are we fulfilling God's intention for us? What about our life together is pleasing to the Lord?

45. *Affirming Bible study: Neh. 13:14*

Nehemiah, who served as governor of Jerusalem a century or so after the return of the Jews from Babylonian captivity, tells of what he did to rebuild Jerusalem and to purify the people of God from persistent sins. Several times he asks God to remember the things he has done out of love for the Lord. Share this verse with your group, and ask them to meditate on it.

"Remember me for this, O my God, and do not blot out what I have so faithfully done for the house of my God and its services."

Then ask everyone to write similar prayers asking God to remember one specific thing they have done out of faithfulness to the Lord.

The prayers should then be read, and a general prayer offered by the leader, thanking God for working in each member to make him more and more faithful and committed.

46. *Affirming Bible study: Ephesians 2:8–10*
These verses tell us that salvation is ours by faith, not rooted in works. But the passage goes on to say that we who have been saved "are God's workmanship, created in Christ Jesus to do good works, which God prepared in advance for us to do."

Ask each to meditate on the verse, and then to list some of the "good works" that Jesus recreated him for. Then share with the group some of the "good works" by which he has showed himself to be God's new creation.

EXPLORATION

A group that meets for ministry comes together to hear the living Word of God. While God's voice is heard both through Scripture and in one another, the written Word of God is critical to the spiritual vitality of such a group. In studying the Bible together, we want to (1) come to understand correctly what a book or passage is saying, and (2) to apply that truth to our own daily experience. Here are some Action Ideas that can be used by a group to dig into the Word of God.

47. *Outline the portion or passage you are studying*

There are a number of ways to outline, but one of the simplest and best is to write a single sentence that summarizes a paragraph or short segment of the section you are studying. For example, here is an outline, in sentence form, of Habakkuk 2.

God seems to be telling Habakkuk that the sinner never really gets away with anything. *Any* sinner. Why?	(2:1–20)
a. The arrogant never has enough; he can't find satisfaction.	(2:1–6)
b. Others are going to pay him back; his actions give them scores to settle!	(2:7, 8)
c. He can never be really secure; his way of life keeps him in danger.	(2:9–11)
d. Only good is going to last; sin and its works will be destroyed in the end.	(2:12–14)
e. (Don't understand this one.)	(2:15–17)
f. Trusting false gods is useless; only God is alive and able to act.	(2:18, 19)

See what a quick and striking "picture of reality" this approach can give!

48. *React*

As you read a passage, argue against it! Jot down all the objections to the picture of reality it seems to be giving. Think really hard to get good objections, then try to answer each one. In the process, you'll gain a surprisingly sharp understanding of what is being said!

For instance, try this technique with Ephesians 5:21–33 if you are in a group of couples.

49. *Paraphrase*

Often the Bible uses familiar phrases and words that may not be used in the context in the way we think of them. When this happens, we're forced to find out what a word or phrase does mean, in context, if we are to understand the passage and glimpse the reality it reveals.

One of the best ways of doing this is to para-phrase—put in our own words (*not* using words in the text, but finding synonyms) the thoughts and sentences of the passage.

For instance, James 2:14–26 uses "faith" and "justified" in ways we have to study to understand. Why not try paraphrasing this passage?

50. *Identification*

One of the most helpful ways of studying the Bible is to identify with a person being talked about or talked to. How does he feel? When have I felt this way? How did he react in the situation? Have I been in similar situations? How did I react? What did God say to this person? What would he be likely to say to me today? The same thing? Something different? Why?

Since the Bible is for living, it is helpful in seeking its picture of reality to enter into the lives of the people whose experiences are recorded for our example!

For instance, read Psalm 74 and see if you have lived through the experiences the psalmist relates.

51. *Word studies*

Often selecting key words and studying them give us insights into a passage. Various tools might be used for such a study, including concordances and lexicons. One helpful approach is to select key words and then try to find the synonym that most accurately restates the thought of the passage.

For example, Ephesians 1:3–14 contains a number of verbs that express God's involvement in our salvation. Make a list of these words, then look for the best synonym for each.

52. *Tone of voice*

Read aloud a passage of Scripture, trying at first to read in an angry, demanding tone, like the one a person might expect from the first mother (p. 57). Then ask another person to read, trying to reflect a tone of voice appropriate to the second mother. Talk together about the differences the tone of voice makes in how group members "hear" the passage.

Talk, too, about how the members have been hearing the Bible and any impact this may have made on their attitude about the Scripture.

A passage you might want to use is Colossians 3:1–10.

53. *Identify and relate*

Select an incident for group study. Spend eight to ten minutes individually thinking about the person(s) the incident involves. Try to understand how each must have felt, and why he did what he did.

Share your understanding of the person(s) and ideas about him (them). Then answer these questions individually: "In what way or ways am I like him? How does what God taught him apply to me now?" Share this with the group and explore together the needs revealed.

(For a developed example of this kind of study, see the plan for group study, pages 94–99.)

Two passages you might enjoy taking this approach with are Mark 1:40–45 and Matthew 16:21–23.

54. *Sharing reality*

Give each group member a 3x5 card on which to write a verse conveying a command or exhortation that usually makes him feel discouraged, inadequate, or guilty because of failure to measure up.

Mix the cards randomly and distribute them so that each group member has someone else's card.

Then, give each person fifteen minutes to *restate* the verse so its nature as reality rather than demand may be seen. Each should also write a brief description of ways in which an experience of that reality might be known.

For instance, a person might write down a verse about witnessing, reflecting his fear to speak to another about Christ. After restating the verse to emphasize it as a statement about the possibility of experiencing reality, another person may give a description like the following: "When you experience this, you don't feel afraid to witness, in fact you don't really even think about it much. It simply begins to seem natural to talk about Jesus when opportunities come. And you don't feel that you need to convert the other person; instead, you just kind of relax and are willing to let God do that. So you don't have to press, or feel pressure."

When all have done this, the group reconvenes. One person first reads the verse, his restatement of it, and the descriptive paragraph he wrote. The others (1) comment on his interpretation, suggesting additions or raising questions and (2) share times when they have actually experienced the reality the verse speaks of.

55. *Thirty-second sharing*

Each person shares a verse of Scripture and explains why that verse is important to him. Each person is limited to thirty seconds for this sharing.

56. *Create a model*

When studying a concept or truth, it is often helpful to have the group try to make a physical model. For instance, if you are studying "the church" or "union with Christ" or "grace," after examining relevant Bible passages set out a box of odds and ends. There can be twine, tacks, paper clips, poker chips, whatever. Using the material in the box, challenge teams of three or four group members to make a model showing how "the church" or "grace" or whatever your theme is expressed in human experience.

When the models have been completed, have each team show and explain its representation to the rest of the group. Many very exciting insights can be gained by such a modeling activity.

57. *A variety of versions*

Encourage your group members to bring a variety of versions when you meet for ministry. Compare the passage you are studying with the different renderings found in the versions. While a paraphrase, such as Phillips or Ken Taylor's *Living Bible* (or *The Word*) can be helpful, remember that the most accurate renderings are found in good translations like the NIV or RSV.

58. *Paper-guided Bible study: John 14–15*

It is often helpful to develop a Bible study that is guided by paper rather than the leader. That is, write out steps for the group to take, give each member a copy of the guide sheet, and then follow the steps together. In such a study, the "leader" has the primary task of keeping the group moving through the steps so the whole study can be completed.

Here is such a study to help a group explore John 14–15.

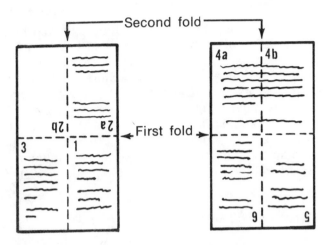

Figure 6	**Figure 7**
Fold paper as shown, with numbered exercises arranged this way.	Reverse side of paper has numbered items arranged as shown.

1. Before beginning the Bible study, think about the self-portraits we have just shared. List the most deeply felt needs that the sharing revealed.

_____

_____

_____

_____

_____

_____

_____

What is your most deeply felt need as you begin this weekend? What do you want most for God to do in your life? (Allow 5 minutes.)

_____

_____

_____

2a. Individually paraphrase in the space on the right the following section of John 15. (Allow 15 minutes.)

"I am the true vine, and my Father is the gardener. He cuts off every branch in me that bears no fruit, while every branch that does bear fruit he trims clean so that it will be even more fruitful. You are already clean because of the word I have spoken to you. Remain in me, and I will remain in you. No branch can bear fruit by itself; it must remain in the vine. I am the vine; you are the branches. If a man remains in me and I in him, he will bear much fruit; apart from me you can do nothing" (John 15:1–5).

2b. From this paragraph, answer:

(1) What do you think "fruit" is? (See Gal. 5:22.)

(2) What is "abiding"? How might we define it?

(3) Is the main thrust of this passage to warn or to promise? Why do you think so?

3. Together, discuss your answers to the questions and read aloud any sections of the paraphrases that seem particularly good or that you have questions about. (Allow 15–20 minutes.)

Then work together to see if you can define what it means to "abide" and what a person does to "abide in Christ." Key verses for your discussion: John 14:15, 21; 15:7, 9, 10. When you have come to an agreement, record your explanation in the space below. (Allow 20 minutes.)

4a and 4b. Read aloud the following passages from the book, *69 Ways to Start a Study Group and Keep It Growing.*

"Love produces obedience. And in obedience the reality of God's presence is made plain.

"It shouldn't be hard to understand this. Sometimes we try to obey out of a sense of duty. Then obedience is a grudging struggle, an attempt to do what we feel God demands of us. But this is always doomed to failure. We're not able to do all we should.

"But sometimes we're moved by love to obey. And what a different focus! Love doesn't think of itself; love fixes its eyes on the loved one. When this happens, we're aware of Jesus, and we discover in amazement that we have done what we could never do before! In forgetting ourselves and thinking of Jesus, we have moved from the *static* to the *dynamic* in life, and we actually experience the reality of Jesus' adequacy.

"There are two realities of our inadequacy: (1) The reality of our inadequacy; (2) The reality of Jesus' adequacy.

"When we concentrate on Jesus and love for him, Jesus fulfills his promise that his disciples will 'keep my words.' In the actual doing of the Word, which requires this divine enabling, we experience God's power.

"Throughout the significant upper room chapters (John 13–17), this thought is emphasized and reemphasized. 'Abide in me,' Jesus encourages. 'Live close to me.' How? 'If you obey my commands, you will remain in my love' (John 15:10).''

Abiding, or "staying close to Jesus," involves
(1) loving him
(2) love-motivated (*not* duty-motivated) obedience

135

(3) experience of Jesus' enablement to live beyond ourselves.

(Take time to discuss the quote and the conclusions before beginning exercise 5.)

5. Reread the John 15 passage again and together list the following: "What evidences can I see here of Jesus' love for me?" "What reasons can I find to love him?" (Think together in depth.)

_____

_____

_____

_____

_____

_____

_____

6. Finally, turn again to exercise 1 and make a list containing all the items each member of the group listed. Then beside each item, agree together on a "fruit" that the Lord promises to produce in us to replace the needs discovered. End your time together by thanking the Lord that he is able to produce fruit, and that he promises to do just this in our lives as we love him and live close to him.

59. *Study Acts 4:23–31 (Concentration)*

Distribute study guides for an exploration of Acts 4:23–31, which will help bring into focus God's power to help the participants realize the ideal. The following sketches and numbered exercises describe the study guide.

NOTE: *Before distributing the study guides, have one person read aloud to the entire group Acts 3:1– 12 and 4:1–22 as background material.*

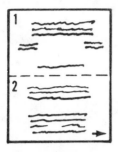

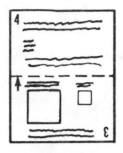

Figure 8

Figure 9

Fold sheet once so that only exercise 1 is visible.

Reverse side shows how exercises 3 and 4 are arranged.

Now go on to the numbered exercises on the following pages. They follow the pattern of the sketches above.

1

From your knowledge about Peter and John as they are portrayed in the Gospels, develop a list of **differences** and **similarities** between them and the Peter and John we see here in Acts. Work together for 15 to 20 minutes to do a careful analysis.

In the Gospels
(before the Resurrection)

In Acts
(after the Resurrection)

(Then turn down to exercise 2.)

Acts 4:23–31 records the response of Peter and John to the challenge. Read and individually UNDERLINE sections that reveal these men's image of God, and CIRCLE sections that reveal their image of themselves (5–8 minutes).

23On their release, Peter and John went back to their own people and reported all that the chief priests and elders had said to them. 24When they heard this, they raised their voices together in prayer to God. "Sovereign Lord," they said, "you made the heaven and the earth and the sea, and everything in them. 25You spoke by the Holy Spirit through the mouth of your servant, our father David:

'Why do the nations rage
and the peoples plot in vain?
26The kings of the earth take their stand
and the rulers gather together
against the Lord
and against the Anointed One.'

27Indeed Herod and Pontius met together with the Gentiles and the people of Israel in this city to conspire against your holy servant Jesus, whom you anointed. 28They did what your power and will had decided beforehand should happen. 29Now, Lord, consider their threats and enable your servants to speak your word with great boldness. 30Stretch out your hand to heal and perform miraculous signs and wonders through the name of your holy servant Jesus."

31After they prayed, the place where they were meeting was shaken. And they were all filled with the Holy Spirit and spoke the word of God boldly.

3

Together, from your study, write in the boxes below words that seem to describe the disciples' view of themselves, and their view of the Lord (15–20 minutes).

John and Peter
saw themselves
as . . .

John and Peter saw God as . . .

4

Complete together:

1. John and Peter were realistic about . . .

2. What seemed most important to John and Peter was not their _____ but God's _____.

3. John and Peter responded to the challenge to live beyond themselves by . . .

    (a)

    (b)

    (c)

    (d)

    (e)

4. The result of their approach to their need for courage and boldness was . . .

Now, together . . .

Apply principles seen in this passage to your own lives. Be aware of your needs, seeing the gap between your ideal self and who you are now. That is, take five minutes to meditate on **what does this mean for me.** Then share your specific applications with the other members of your small group.

60. *Key word*

There are brief approaches to studying a passage that also enable us to get at the heart of its teaching. Have each group member read the passage to be studied and select a *key word*. Then in discussion each tells the key word, tells what it means in that passage, and how that key word helps each to understand what God is saying in that section.

61. *Key verse*

Use the same approach as with a key-word study. Have group members select what seems to be the key verse of a passage. Explain what it means, how it sums up the teaching of the passage, and what we are to learn from the passage itself.

62. *Coding*

Develop a simple coding system for your group members to use in studying a passage, such as dots, check marks, initials, etc. The code symbol should be placed in the margin beside a verse.

Here are some of the things you might want to code:

- teaching about God
- teaching about the Christian life
- teaching about relationship with God
- teaching about relationships with others

The things you code might vary with the Bible book or the passage being explored by the group.

63. *Dramatize*

Have teams develop a short one-scene play. A Bible passage can be dramatized in a variety of ways. Narratives can be represented directly, with lines added to what is reported in Scripture to express implied feelings and thoughts of participants.

Dramas can focus on other elements; for instance, a scene can represent a situation that led Paul to write a particular passage in one of his letters. Or it can represent what happened when a New Testament letter was received by a local congregation.

64. *Debate*

It's often helpful to explore differences Christians have concerning biblical teaching, not to determine who is "right," but to try to understand different points of view.

When there is a difficult passage, poll your group members to see which "side" they take. Then assign two or four *to represent the other side* next session in a brief debate.

After the "debate," rather than vote on who "won," talk with the debaters. What did each learn in studying the passage? In studying the "other side"? What fresh insights were gained?

65. *Quizdown*

Divide into teams, each of which is to develop a list of ten questions about a passage the group has studied. The questions are not to be "trick" or "trivia" questions, but to focus on significant issues in the passage.

After studying the passage and developing the best set of questions possible, let teams ask and answer each other's questions. Both the process of study to develop their own questions and the process of trying to answer the other team's will ensure a mastery of the content.

66. *Study books*

Study books can be helpful to a group that meets for ministry. It's generally best to choose books that *help you explore Scripture* rather than books *about* Scripture.

What are qualities to look for in good Bible study materials?

● They focus on a passage, rather than string isolated verses together.

● They suggest thought and application questions, not just "look up a fact" questions.

● They suggest discussion and other group activities, rather than limit themselves to what an individual might do alone.

CONCENTRATION

As we meet for ministry, we want to be especially sensitive to what Jesus is doing in each of our lives. This has two aspects: We want to listen for his voice, and see how he is calling each of us to experience the living Word of God. What is typically called "application" of Scripture thus becomes a major element in our gathering. We also want to be sensitive to what Jesus *is* doing in each other's lives. We want to encourage sharing of our personal experience with the Lord.

Here are Action Ideas that will help a group apply Scripture and share what Jesus is doing in each life.

67. *Portraits of Jesus*
Have various members of your group share how they see Jesus, and tie in their portraits either to Scripture or to their personal experiences of his love. There are many variations to this approach. Your group may select a gospel incident and examine how the disciples might have seen Jesus. Or the crowd. Or Satan (a very disgruntled onlooker!).

144

68. *Memorization*

A verse like Colossians 1:16 ("all created by him and for him") may be assigned for memorization and meditation. When the group assembles, do what the class described in the chapter did. Each completed the statement: "I was made for Jesus to . . ." and shared one way in which they realized they were made for him and could glorify him.

69. *Focused Bible study*

Select a passage of Scripture and focus on what it reveals about the Lord and his relationship to you. For instance, here is part of a study guide to Ephesians used in a small group in Phoenix, Arizona.

List the verbs in Ephesians 1:3–14 that tell what God has done in providing salvation, and beside each give a synonym which seems to best restate the idea.

_____   _____

_____   _____

_____   _____

_____   _____

_____   _____

_____   _____

_____   _____

_____   _____

_____   _____

Record which of these activities best communicates a sense of God's love for you. Why?

70. *Jesus in me this week*

How have we seen Jesus in our lives this week? This is a basic question and ought to provide a central element in sharing each time a group meets. Rehears ing what the Lord has done in us and for us is the heart of building awareness of Jesus and who he is for us.

71. *Giving gifts*

As needs are expressed or shared, a group may stop and have each member give, in Jesus' name, a particular gift to the person who has expressed concern. The goal is for each to try to see the person sharing as Jesus sees him, and then to communicate what the Lord is able to do in his life.

For instance, one group member might share frustration in working with another person in her office and the tears that come at home after another day of tension and bickering. The other group members might then begin to give gifts—the kind of gifts Jesus is eager and willing and able to give.

—"Ruth, in Jesus' name, I want to give you a peaceful spirit, to quiet the upset you feel."

—"Ruth, in Jesus' name, I want to give you a forgiving spirit, to wash out some of the bitterness that must be building up."

—"Ruth, in Jesus' name, I want to give you a loving spirit, to overcome the negativism there and reach out to help the other person, who must be hurting too."

Giving gifts may be done at any time in a group meeting, or it may be a part of the group's life, planned for every third or fourth session as a regular feature.

72. *Identifying God's voice*

After Bible study, ask those who have been able to hear God's voice speaking to them share what Jesus communicated and how they intend to respond to him.

146

It is important to help our group members realize that when we meet for ministry, we do not gather simply to learn "about" Jesus, but to listen for his personal guidance and to plan to respond to his leading.

Each group member may not hear a personal message each week, but as those who do share, each will become more sensitive and ready to listen to the Lord.

73. *Encouraging accountability*

When you meet for ministry, ask for reports from those who said they heard God's voice the week before and intended to respond to him. These will both encourage others and help them sense Christ's presence, as well as motivate response in those who hear the Lord, knowing they will be accountable to share how they responded to God's voice.

74. *In his steps*

Peter reminds us that as Christians we have been called to "follow in his [Jesus'] steps" (1 Peter 2:22).

After studying a Bible passage, talk (1) about how Jesus actually practiced that truth while here on earth, and (2) how Jesus might put it into practice if he lived in our time.

75. *Varied application*

Most Bible truths can be applied in a number of ways in our lives and relationships. However, all too often we limit our vision by focusing on just one or two ways that a passage relates to modern Christian life.

After a Bible study, it's often helpful to brainstorm (list without evaluating) as many as possible different applications of what has been studied.

As varied applications are listed, we can trust the Holy Spirit to speak to individuals in our group to call them to the specific response the Lord wishes each to make.

76. *Written commitment*

At the end of a study, ask each person to write out a personal commitment defining how he will respond to what Jesus has said in the Word. Give each an envelope and stamp. The written commitment should be sealed inside the envelope and the person's own address written on it, so it can be mailed. When the letter comes during the week, it will be a reminder of the commitment, as well as a method of self-check.

77. *Support partners*

It is often helpful to have a partner in the group. The partner should *not* be a spouse. Each should contact his partner at least once during the week to share what's happening, prayer requests, and how he has been able to respond to the Lord.

78. *Practice Jesus' presence*

Take time as the meeting begins to welcome Jesus. The Bible promises that where even two or three are gathered in Christ's name, he is among them. Consciously and verbally welcome the Lord to your gathering, asking him to participate not only by listening to what each says but also by speaking through the members and his Word.

You may even wish to have an ''empty'' chair that each realizes is Christ's chair, thus symbolizing his real presence among you.

79. *Meeting Jesus in Scripture: Luke 21:1–4*

Select a brief incident to look at together, just to

sense something special about Jesus. For instance, in this passage, Christ comments about a widow's gift of two "very small copper coins" and compares her gift to that of those who give thousands.

Read such a passage and meditate on what it says to each of you about Jesus. Then in turn say, "Jesus, who is with us, . . ." and complete the sentence with an insight gained from the incident.

Pray, thanking the Lord for joining you that evening.

80. *Meeting Jesus in Scripture: Matthew 5:43–48*

Read a quote of Jesus' words from one of the Gospels, like the words found in Matthew 5:43–48. Ask each person to meditate on them, and to think of a time when Jesus might have been most likely to speak these words personally.

Share the time and explain why Jesus would have spoken those words just then.

Ask the Lord to make your group members aware the next time these specific words should be heard by each in an individual situation.

81. *Meeting Jesus in Scripture: Matthew 8:18–22*

Read a short section in which Jesus interacts with another person. Ask each person to think about that incident silently. Then share these answers: What do I learn about my own personal relationship with Jesus from this incident? How is Jesus calling me to respond to him? What is he saying to me, personally?

82. *Meeting Jesus in Scripture: Matthew 9:27–31*

Read a short section describing one of Jesus' miracles. Ask each to meditate on the incident. Then share these answers: What in my life, just now, corresponds to the need Jesus met? How will his power be expressed in me as it was in the person(s) Jesus served then? What do I need to do to appropriate this power in my own life, and experience Jesus more directly?

83. *Reflecting*

The Bible says that as we experience inner transformation by the Spirit of God, we more and more reflect Jesus in our lives (2 Cor. 3:18).

When appropriate, take time to share this answer: How is Jesus being expressed in the lives of those who meet for ministry? Let your group members share with each other "ways in which I see Jesus in your life."

84. *Imaging*

Jesus lived on earth as a perfect man, always doing the will of the Father. His perfection still attracts us and exemplifies the beauty we want to see in our own character.

After studying a passage, ask each to think what quality of Jesus is most closely related to its application in our own life. For instance, one person may feel that Jesus' power is what he needs. Another may think of Jesus' compassion, his willingness to sacrifice himself, his submission to the Father, etc.

After each has identified the quality of Jesus that seems to be most closely related to putting that week's Word from God into practice, ask each to close his eyes and image Jesus not just present *beside* but *within* him.

Image Jesus growing in size to fill his body, thoughts, life.

The Bible teaches that we have a real union with Jesus. As we acknowledge that union, and visualize him within us with all his traits available to us, we will be strengthened to respond obediently and to live as he lived in our world.

85. *Liturgy*

The early church used liturgy to remind its members of who Jesus is, and what his presence means. Two biblical passages that many believe had this liturgical use are Philippians 2:5–11 and Colossians 1:13–20.

Use one of these passages weekly as you gather, reading it together or responsively, as you focus not simply on Jesus' presence but also on who he truly is.

ADORATION

Our first and perhaps most significant response to God as he reveals himself to us is worship. Here are Action Ideas that you can use to affirm God and to worship and praise him when you meet for ministry.

86. *Songs*

Build a repertoire of simple, short worship songs and hymns. For several weeks, teach a new song as the meeting opens. Then, with the music held in common, any member of the group can start a known song when moved to praise. (Do *not* use song sheets in your meetings; they tend to limit spontaneity.)

87. *Testimony*

Address your sharing to the Lord, speaking directly to him: "I praise you, Lord, for . . ." and continue to express something the Lord has done in your life the previous week.

88. *Prayer*

Pattern prayer on Psalms:

Select an appropriate praise psalm (cf. Ps. 66, 93,

96, 98, 100, 105, 111, and others) to use in one of the
following ways:

— Pray a verse in unison, then pause to let
   individuals add their own thoughts and praises
   before continuing to the next.
— After sharing, select a few verses of a praise
   psalm to paraphrase, building in the experiences
   of the group members that have been shared.
   Read as prayers several of these paraphrases,
   and use them at home during the week to praise
   the Lord.
— Select praise verses from the Book of Psalms
   for memorization by the group.
— Discuss a psalm in depth, exploring the portrait
   of God it expresses and the works of God that
   have led to praise, relating all to our lives today.
— Write a modern-day psalm together, stressing a
   particular theme (God's goodness, power, some
   blessing).

Spontaneous prayer

Group members should be free to introduce prayer
and praise to God at any time during the session.
Spontaneous prayer may be of a short, interjectory
nature—simply a "Thank you, Lord" or a longer
expression of praise and thanksgiving. Often groups
will not develop this practice because it seems
unusual (and thus uncomfortable for some) at first.
Yet spontaneous prayers can help the group realize
the immediate presence of the Lord—he *is* where the
two or three are gathered! Spontaneous prayers can
also help each person develop a sensitivity to the
Lord's presence that will carry over into his daily life
and lead to expressions of praise during the day and
week.

To help the group feel comfortable in being involved in spontaneous prayer and praise experiences: (1) Talk over the whole idea as a group, thinking together of the values and discussing freely any hesitation members might have. (2) Plan to try spontaneous prayer for two sessions of the group meeting, encouraging members as they feel thankful to lead the group in expressing thanks right then. At first, this will seem artificial, but it may lead to a truly spontaneous expression of worship and praise. (3) Select a praise leader for each session and ask him to be sensitive to times when the group seems ready to praise the Lord or when it has shared experiences that naturally might lead to praise. After several weeks, no praise leader should be needed to keep the group aware of the Lord; all will be sensitized to his presence.

89. *Communion*

While some groups may feel that Communion should not be held without an ordained minister to lead, others have felt free to close a meeting with the breaking of bread. Communion is a joyful and yet solemn act of shared worship—an affirmation of Jesus as Savior and Lord and an evidence of commitment to him until he comes again.

To hold Communion in a small group, read together (or appoint a member to read) 1 Corinthians 11:23–28. Pass around a common loaf, from which each breaks a piece, and pass paper cups of juice. Prayer over the elements and praise to the Lord may be offered by members of the group as they will.

90. *A worship session*

Look at the simple plan for worship on the next two pages.

1. Meditate on this prayer, then record your insights along each margin. (Allow 20 minutes.)

In my own words . . .

What does God want and intend to do for me?

(record here)

A prayer for me

That out of his glorious riches he may strengthen you with power through his Spirit in your inner being so that Christ may dwell in your hearts through faith. And I pray that you, being rooted and established in love, may have power, together with all the saints, to grasp how wide and long and high and deep is the love of Christ and to know this love that surpasses knowledge—that you may be filled to the measure of all the fullness of God. Now to him who is able to do immeasurably more than all we ask or imagine, according to his power that is at work within us, to him be glory in the church and in Christ Jesus throughout all generations, for ever and ever! Amen.

Ephesians 3:16–21

In my own words . . .

How can I be sure he will do this in me?

(record here)

2. How can you express your praise to God? (Allow 30–40 minutes.)

   Select one verse or phrase from the Scripture passage that is most meaningful to you, and express your praise in one of the following ways, or in some other creative way:

   a. Make a poster.
   b. Write your own psalm.
   c. Write a chorus or a song to sing.
   d. Write a prayer poem.
   e. Plan a pantomime.
   f. Find a hymn that expresses your feelings.
   g. Draw or paint a picture.

3. Come together for a worship time. (Allow 30–60 minutes.)

   Let each person share what was most meaningful in the passage and why; then use what he has created to lead the others in worship of the Lord.

91. *Praise time*

Organize praise time around two themes, expressed both in spontaneously begun songs and vocalized prayers and praise. The themes, which may be introduced by two posters, are

Let us praise God for who he is

Let us praise God for what he has done in us

92. *Quaker meeting*

Let everyone know they will have the opportunity to share from their quiet time and learnings of the week. You may want to ask two or three to prepare longer, ten-minute studies or devotionals. But the meeting should be open for all to participate in, to share from Scripture, to encourage, rebuke, exhort, teach, or testify.

93. *Choral praise*

Divide into two equal groups to read alternately the verses of Psalm 136, which praise God and recall his steadfast lovingkindness.

94. *Offering our best*

What does each person in the group do best? Perhaps it's singing; perhaps, playing tennis. Maybe it's baking, or writing poetry, or growing flowers. Whatever it may be, ask each person to identify it and then during the next few weeks, determine how to offer that "best" to the Lord.

The offering of one's best may be done in private, although it should be reported to the group, or may be done in the group itself. But each should be seen by the person as worship, as giving praise and thanks to God for what he has done first in giving the particular talent or ability to the individual.

95. *Alternate worship leadership*

For every meeting ask a different person to conclude the gathering by leading a time of worship. Each should be encouraged to build around a particular trait of God that is associated with what you are studying—God's goodness, mercy, love, faithfulness, justice, longsuffering, etc.

There should be no set pattern for the worship, but it may include readings, songs, prayers, etc., as the worship leader chooses. The one overarching criterion is this: The individual should lead the others to actively worship the Lord.

96. *Develop group liturgies*

Liturgy has been used in Christian worship from biblical times. The Song of Moses (Exodus 15), the psalms, and many liturgical sections in the Epistles make it clear that carefully planned expressions of faith and appreciation can be meaningful for us, and for God.

If you have a person gifted in liturgy, ask that person to write a brief liturgy associated with the topic you are exploring together when you meet for ministry.

(Typical "liturgy" even in nonliturgical churches is represented in a church's call to worship, in the responsive reading, and the quoting of the Lord's Prayer or Apostle's Creed.)

97. *Experiencing God*

As a brief worship experience, emphasize an aspect of God's nature or character related to what you have been reading in Scripture. Again, any quality—grace, mercy, judgment, kindness, or patience—is appropriate.

This time, ask each to share how that quality or

attribute of the Lord has been experienced, and then
address a brief sentence prayer of thanks to him.

98. *Response to in-person revelation*

As another shares, don't hesitate to stop and lead
the group in praise. Thank the Lord for what he is
doing in or through the brother or sister, and express
the whole group's appreciation of this evidence of
God's presence and power.

99. *Books*

Continue looking in Christian bookstores for books
that will enrich your understanding of meeting for
ministry and will stimulate a flow of fresh ideas to
maintain those vital processes that make small-group
meetings such a wonderful opportunity for spiritual
growth.